The Faith of a British-Israelite

By
THE REV. ALBAN HEATH

THE COVENANT PUBLISHING COMPANY LIMITED
121, Low Etherley, Bishop Auckland, Co. Durham DL14 0HA

2009

FIRST EDITION 1935

SECOND EDITION 1962

THIRD EDITION REVISED 2008

2009

ISBN-978-0-85205-043-9

Printed by
THE COVENANT PUBLISHING COMPANY LIMITED
121, Low Etherley, Bishop Auckland,
Co. Durham DL14 0HA

www.covpub.co.uk

Cover photography by John Battersby.

DEDICATION

TO MY DEAR WIFE

IN

GROWING APPRECIATION

PREFACE TO 2008 EDITION

This revised edition has had some of the footnotes and text updated to take into account historical changes since the original text was written.

The Covenant Publishing Company Ltd.

FOREWORD

WHAT British-Israelites believe has been so much distorted by the uninformed that it seemed good to present a simpler and condensed statement of the fundamentals of our faith. British-Israelites believe and accept the whole Bible, and all Bible truth is B-I truth. In the following pages I have tried to set forth in concise form the tenets of our faith and teaching, with particular reference to the distinctive aspects of our message. We ask that the Bible be read naturally, as any other book would be read, in the firm belief that God says what He means and means what He says. I remember the late F.B. Meyer advising an audience to stop for a time the use of the words "In the name of Jesus Christ our Lord." He was trying to drive home the lesson that familiarity with the term blinds us to its significance. In the same way, we ask readers of the Bible to allow the Word to come as God's message to the individual, to the nation, and to the world.

THE AUTHOR

THE FAITH OF A BRITISH-ISRAELITE

1

WE BELIEVE GOD. Not only do we believe in God, we believe God. "Abraham believed God, and it was counted unto him for righteousness" (Romans 4:3). In a time of threatened calamity, St. Paul said, "I believe God" (Acts 27:25). Both Abraham and St. Paul had heard a voice. They believed that voice was the voice of God. They believed what was said to them and acted accordingly. In the case of St. Paul his obedience to the spoken word resulted in saving 276 lives.

In a similar way we believe God. We accept as true and binding whatever God says. The Bible records many instances where God spoke, e.g. "God spake all these words, saying..." (Exodus 20: 1). Although we may not always understand all that He says we still believe God. Within the limits of metaphorical speech, we refuse to believe that God said one thing and meant another. We cannot conceive of God using words to deceive the people who trust in Him. We believe that God can and will fulfil all His promises even though, to our unenlightened eyes, it may seem impossible to do so. With Abraham and St. Paul we say, we believe God.

2

WE BELIEVE THE BIBLE IS THE WORD OF GOD. Many good and earnest people say the Bible *contains* the Word of God. To them, the Bible is like the curate's egg: it is good in parts. We believe the whole Bible, both the Old Testament and the New Testament. We believe it would be impossible for any human being or for any number of human beings to produce such a book as the Bible by human means alone. The nature, the scope and accuracy of its contents stamp the Bible as a Book of more than human origin.

We accept the Old Testament as the Word of God. There are very many references to the Old Testament in the New Testament, none of which ever questions the authenticity and authority of the Old Testament. The Old Testament was the only Bible our Lord and His Disciples possessed. When Christ or the early Christians speak of the Scriptures it is to what we call the Old Testament that they refer. They are unanimous in their verdict that the Old Testament was accepted as the Word of God. "All Scripture is given by inspiration of God and is profitable for doctrine, for reproof, for correction, for instruction in righteousness, that the man of God may be perfect, thoroughly furnished unto all good works" (2 *Timothy* 2:17). "For whatsoever things were written aforetime were written for our learning, that we through patience and comfort of the Scriptures might have hope" (*Romans* 15: 4). Here we see that St. Paul found in the Old Testament not only a basis for his religious belief but, also, a guide for his everyday conduct.

Our Lord accepted the Old Testament without question. To the Jews of His day He said "Search the Scriptures; for in them ye think ye have eternal life: and they are they which testify of me" (*John* 5:39). In the days of His flesh He frequently made use of Old Testament words and always quoted them with approval. He never said they were wrong. After His resurrection He made comprehensive reference to the whole of the Old Testament and set the seal of His approval upon it. The Hebrew Bible is divided into three sections: the Law, the Prophets, and the Sacred Writings or Scriptures. In His talk on the way to Emmaus, "Beginning at Moses, and all the prophets, he expounded to them in all the Scriptures [sacred writings] the things concerning Himself" (*Luke* 24: 27).

Here we see that our Lord set His seal upon the Old Testament in its threefold division. "It is enough for the disciple that he be as his master, and the servant as his lord" (*Matthew* 10:25). We are in the best of company when we join our Lord in a reverent acceptance of the Old Testament as the Word of God.

To some, the New Testament presents problems of its own, but it presents no material difficulties to those who accept it as an inspired production. "God, who at sundry times and in divers manners spake in times past unto the fathers by the prophets, hath in these last days spoken unto us by *His* Son" (*Hebrews* 1:1). We have records of His spoken words in the Gospels. These were uttered in the days of His flesh. But we have other words of our Lord given after His resurrection. The last book in the New Testament, *Revelation*, opens with words which should never have been misunderstood: "The Revelation of Jesus Christ which God gave unto him, to shew to his servants things which must shortly come to pass; and he sent and signified *it* by his angel unto his servant John: who bare record of the word of God, and of the testimony of Jesus Christ, and of all things that he saw" (*Revelation* 1:1-2). John claims nothing more than the office of scribe. The Revelation is from God to His Son, our Lord, thence from Jesus Christ to an angel who passes it on to John. In the *Book of Revelation* God is speaking through His Son to His servants. It is God's word, and we believe it even though we may not understand it.

One of the promises of Jesus was that the Holy Spirit would lead His disciples into the way of all truth. This is often applied to believers in all times. That may be a reasonable inference, but it is not so stated in the text. After saying what the Holy Spirit would do to and for the world (*John* 16:7-11), our Lord proceeds to say what the Holy Spirit would do for the disciples whom He was addressing (*John* 16:12-15). "This section distinctly marks the position of the apostles with regard to revelation as unique; and so by implication the office of the apostolic writings as a record of their teaching."[1] Our Lord says of the Holy Spirit in relation to the apostles, "He shall glorify me: for he shall receive of mine, and show it unto you" (v 14). The New Testament writings are the record of the truth given, or recalled, to the

---

[1] *Gospel of St. John.* Bishop B.F. Westcott, (Macmillan, London, 1881). Section 16:12-25

apostles by the Holy Spirit concerning our Lord. The New Testament is therefore the Word of God, and we believe it and accept it as such. St. Peter refers to the writings of St. Paul in these words: "Even as our beloved brother Paul also *according to the wisdom given unto him* hath written unto you; as also in all *his* epistles, speaking in them of these things; in which are some things hard to be understood, which they that are unlearned and unstable wrest, as they do also *the other scriptures,* unto their own destruction" (2 *Peter* 3: 15-16). Note the words I have thrown into italics. Paul's wisdom was given unto him. Note also the implied comparison between the scriptures by St. Paul and the other scriptures. "Holy men of God spake as they were moved by the Holy Ghost" (2 *Peter* 1: 21).

4

WE BELIEVE IN THE CHURCH as a divinely constituted and divinely commissioned body. The last two verses of *St. Matthew's Gospel* define its mandate and specify its commission. "Go ye therefore, and teach all nations, baptising them in the name of the Father, and of the Son, and of the Holy Ghost; teaching them to observe all things whatsoever I have commanded you: and, lo, I am with you alway, *even* unto the end of the world." In the English translation given above two distinct Greek words are translated by the word *teach*. The first Greek word means *make disciples*, and is so rendered in the margin, while the second Greek word means instruct, or teach in the ordinary meaning of that word. Moffatt renders the passage "Go and make disciples of all nations... and teach them to obey all the commands I have laid on you." The constituency to which such instruction is to be given is *all nations*, and the subject matter of the instruction to be given is *whatsoever I have commanded you.* The subject matter of our Lord's teaching was the Kingdom of God. He began His public ministry by declaring "The Kingdom of God is at hand" (*Mark* 1: 15).

Most of His Parables deal with the Kingdom of God. On the eve of His crucifixion He assured His friends that He would not henceforth drink of the fruit of the vine until He drank it new with them in the Father's Kingdom (*Matthew* 26:29). Between His Resurrection and Ascension, on various occasions, "He showed Himself alive" to His disciples "speaking of the things pertaining to the Kingdom of God" (*Acts* 1: 3). He declared, "This Gospel of the Kingdom shall be preached in all the world for a witness to all nations; and then shall the end come" (*Matthew* 24:14). Since the commission to the Church was to teach the nations "to obey all the commands I have laid on you," and since He commanded that the Gospel of the Kingdom was to be preached in all the world for a witness to all nations, it follows that the mission of the Church is to preach and teach the Gospel of the Kingdom. The Church is not an end in itself; it is a means to an end, the end being the Kingdom of God.

There is no scriptural warrant for regarding the Church and the Kingdom as identical. The Kingdom is a much bigger thing than the Church. The Kingdom is all inclusive, and embraces the Church, but the term Church cannot be made to cover and include the Kingdom. The Church's evangel is to the individual, while the Gospel of the Kingdom is, as shown above, clearly and definitely addressed to *nations*. As an organised nation affects the whole life of the community, social, economic, political, and religious, so the Kingdom of God is inclusive of all that relates to the physical, moral, and spiritual welfare of the community. Professor Hort, one of the most learned men the Church of England has produced, pointed out that we are not justified in regarding the Church and the Kingdom as identical: "Since Augustine's time the Kingdom of Heaven or Kingdom of God, of which we read so often in the Gospels, has been simply identified with the Christian Ecclesia. This is a not unnatural deduction from some of our Lord's sayings on the subject taken by themselves; but it cannot, I think, hold its ground when the whole range of His teaching about it is comprehensively examined. We may speak of the Ecclesia as the visible representative of the Kingdom of God, or as the primary instrument of its sway, or under any other analogous forms of language, but we are not justified in identifying the one with the other, so as to be able to apply directly to the Ecclesia whatever is said in the Gospels about the Kingdom of Heaven or of God."[2]

Equally so, there is no scriptural basis for the teaching that the Church is the Bride of Christ. According to the teaching of the New Testament the Church is the body of Christ. "Know ye not that your bodies are the members of Christ?" (1 *Corinthians* 6:15). "Now ye are the body of Christ, and members in particular" (1 *Corinthians* 12:27). Again St. Paul writes of "the Church, which is His body" (*Ephesians* 1:23). It is a physical impossibility for a man to marry his own body and it would be straining language beyond all legitimate use to say Christ as the Bridegroom is to marry "the Church, which is His body." We interpret these and other related Scriptures as meaning that Christ with the members of His body is the Bridegroom, and that the Marriage Supper of the Lamb (*Revelation* 19:4-9), adumbrates the union of the Bridegroom with the true Israel of God for the proper functioning of the Kingdom of God on earth. Under the old dispensation God declares to Israel: "I am married to you" (*Jeremiah* 3:14). Israel, as an unfaithful wife, was divorced from God (*Hosea* 1 and 2). God would lure her into the wilderness where she would be re-united with her "first husband," and God declares, "I will betroth thee unto me for ever." The ideal union is not between God and particular individuals but between God and His holy nation.

The relation of the body to the soul is a metaphysical problem with which the ancient philosophers liked to grapple. Is the soul like the music produced from an instrument by the agent, man, or is the body like a boat propelled and directed by the power of the rower? Without going into the subtleties

---

[2] *The Christian Ecclesia: A course Of Lectures on the Early History and Early Conceptions of The Ecclesia, and One Sermon.* Prof. F.J.A. Hort, D.D; LL.D; D.C.L.(Macmillan, London, 1914) p.19.

of these arguments we can affirm that the body enables the thoughts and intentions of the heart to find expression. The members of the body are the errand boys of the soul carrying its messages. So, we conceive, "The Church, which is His body," should be at the disposal of Christ to enable Him to transmit His messages and to give effect to His will.

5

WE ACCEPT AND BELIEVE THE GREAT CREEDS OF THE CHURCH, and we accept and believe them without mental reservations. We believe the Church, under the guidance of the Holy Spirit, was led to formulate the articles of Christian belief in terms that are plain to all people. Nor can we be persuaded that the Creeds affirm one thing but mean another. When the Creeds declare that our Lord was born of the Virgin Mary we understand the words to mean that He came into the world not by ordinary means of procreation but through a special intervention of God Himself. We accept without demur or question the statement of "The angel of the Lord" to Joseph, when questions of propriety were disturbing the serenity of his heart and mind, "That which is conceived [begotten] in her is of the Holy Ghost" (*Matthew* 1:20). Such things are clearly beyond the range of human understanding, but the Creeds do not call upon us to declare that we understand them; we are asked to affirm that we believe and not that we understand. In our everyday life we believe many things we do not understand. It should be borne in mind that the word *believe* means not merely intellectual assent: it means *live by*. In other words, to believe, in its original sense, means to shape one's life in agreement with the things we affirm to be true.

When the Creeds call upon us to say, "I believe... that He shall come again to judge the quick and the dead," we understand the words to mean that the Church calls upon us to affirm as a fact of Christian belief that our Lord will come again in the plain, literal meaning of the word *come*. We readily make such an affirmation because it is in strict agreement with the teaching of Holy Scripture. In the simplest and plainest language our Lord declared, "I will come again" (*John* 14:3). The angels told the disciples, "This same Jesus, which is taken up from you into heaven, shall so come in like manner as ye have seen Him go into heaven" (*Acts* 1:11).

When the Creeds affirm that our Lord "shall come to judge the quick and the dead," they do but state in other terms what our Lord Himself said, "For the Father judgeth no man, but hath committed all judgement to the Son... and hath given Him authority to execute judgement also, because He is the Son of man" (*John* 5:22-27). We give to this article of Christian belief our full, free, and ready assent without any qualifying "if" or "but," and we seek to shape our lives in expectation of the personal return of our Lord to this earth.

6

WE BELIEVE THAT THE COVENANTS recorded in the Bible represent God's plan for the world and His unfailing purposes for His children. We regard THE FOUR MAJOR COVENANTS as the warp around which the whole fabric of divine purpose is woven. Jeremiah speaks of God's covenant of the day and night (*Jeremiah* 33:20-25), and there is the covenant of which the rainbow is the token (*Genesis* 9:12-17), but the four major Covenants to which we refer are:

> The Covenant with Abraham,
> The Covenant with Israel through Moses,
> The Covenant with David,
> The new Covenant in Christ Jesus.

First in order of time is THE COVENANT WITH ABRAHAM. This was an unconditional covenant. There are no "ifs" and no "buts" attached to it. God did not say He would do this if Abraham did, or would do, that, nor did He say this would take place but Abraham must not do that. In the simplest and most direct language God made a definite pronouncement (*Genesis* 12:1-3) which, later, He confirmed and amplified on oath, (*Genesis* 22:16-18). Both the Old Testament and the New Testament are at pains to stress the fact that God's declaration was made on oath. An oath, the dictionary tells us, is "a solemn statement with an appeal to God as witness, and a calling for His vengeance in case of falsehood or failure." In taking an oath, we swear by someone greater than ourselves, but since there is no one greater than God He could not swear an oath as we do. The Scriptures are clear and emphatic on the procedure followed:

> "By Myself have I sworn, saith the Lord" (*Genesis* 22:16). "For when God made promise to Abraham, because He could sware by no greater, He sware by Himself... For men verily sware by the greater... Wherein God, willing more abundantly to shew unto the heirs of promise the immutability of His counsel, confirmed it by an oath" (*Hebrews* 6:13-17).

In law, an oath is "an appeal [in verification of a statement made] to a superior sanction, in such a form as exposes the party making the appeal to an indictment for perjury if the statement be false," and perjury "at common law [is] a wilfully false statement in a fact material to the issue, made by a witness under oath in a competent judicial proceeding".

British-Israelites are not prepared to charge God with perjury, for "God is not a man, that he should lie" (*Numbers* 23:19).

A covenant, the dictionary tells us, is "a mutual agreement," or, in another sense, "the writing containing the agreement." It is sometimes objected that since Abraham was not asked to assent to the terms of the Covenant it was not "a *mutual* agreement," and for that reason it was not strictly a covenant: it was a Divine promise. The Bible itself frequently refers to the promise made to Abraham, and to Isaac and

Jacob, but it also uses the term *covenant* to express the relationship existing. God says to Abraham, "I will make my covenant between Me and thee" (verse 4). St. Paul uses both terms in *Galatians* 3:17. That it was a promise made by God is beyond question, and many passages of Scripture become clearer if we bear that in mind.

7

If we dig deeper into the roots of the term *covenant* we see not only its fuller meaning but, also, justification for its use in this connection. The word "covenant" is derived from two Latin words, *con*, together, and *venio*, to come. It therefore expresses that relation in which two people come together in mutual agreement. While Abraham was not asked to give any verbal assent to the agreement, he gave tacit consent by his actions. 'Actions speak louder than words.' He responded to the call to leave his native land (*Genesis* 11:1-4) by an act of obedience. "By faith, Abraham when he was called to go out into a place which he should after receive for an inheritance, obeyed, and he went out, not knowing whither he went" (*Hebrews* 11: 8). The fuller Covenant is explicitly associated with a further act of faith on the part of Abraham. "God did tempt [test] Abraham... Take now thy son, thine only son Isaac... and offer him... for a burnt offering" (*Genesis* 22:1-2). "By faith Abraham, when he was tried, offered up Isaac: and he that had received the promises offered up his only begotten" (*Hebrews* 11:17). His willingness to trust God to this degree led to the divine pronouncement on oath (*Genesis* 22:16). As a result of these noble actions of faith Abraham and God came together in an irrevocable Covenant.

The Covenant with Abraham was made centuries before the Law was given, but was neither cancelled nor superseded by the enactments on Sinai. St. Paul stresses this in his *Epistle to the Galatians*, "Now this I say: a covenant confirmed beforehand by God, the law, which came four hundred and thirty years after, doth not disannul, so as to make the promise of none effect" (*Galatians* 3:17 RV). "Though it be but a man's covenant, yet if it be confirmed, no man disannulleth, or addeth thereto" (verse 15, AV). The whole drift of his argument is this: whatever happened subsequent to the Covenant with Abraham could not be in conflict with God's original promise; it could be only an outworking of the terms of the Covenant, or an application of the principles embodied therein. The Covenant with Abraham is the foundation on which rests the whole of Israel history. "For the gifts and calling of God *are* without repentance," or, as Moffatt renders the passage, "For God never goes back upon His gifts and call" (*Romans* 11:29). We see, then, that the Covenant with Abraham remains a permanent promise and is valid for all time. It is described as "His holy covenant: the oath which he sware to our forefather Abraham" (*Luke* 1:73), and "an everlasting covenant." (*Genesis* 17:7). To suggest that this Covenant has been cancelled, or transferred, is tantamount to saying God has gone back on His word and has failed in His promise.

St. Paul stresses also the fact that the Covenant blessings are not contingent on circumcision. The blessings promised to Abraham were announced a quarter of a century before the act of circumcision took place.[3] "Faith was reckoned to Abraham for righteousness. How then was it reckoned? When he was in circumcision, or in uncircumcision? Not in circumcision, but in uncircumcision" (*Romans* 4:10). "He only got circumcision as a sign or seal of the righteousness which belonged to his faith as an uncircumcised man" (Moffatt, verse 11). The argument that the heirs to the promise made to Abraham must be a people practising the rite of circumcision is found, therefore, to be without foundation.

---

[3] Abraham was seventy-five when he left Haran (*Genesis* 12:4); he was ninety-nine when he was circumcised (*Genesis* 17:24).

8

The terms of the Covenant with Abraham are full and explicit, though they grow in fullness and clarity with the passing of the years. The original promise is recorded in *Genesis* 12:1-3:

> "Now the Lord had said unto Abraham, get thee out of thy country, and from thy kindred, and from thy father's house, unto a land that I will shew thee: and I will make of thee a great nation, and I will bless thee, and make thy name great, and thou shalt be a blessing: and I will bless them that bless thee, and curse him that curseth thee: and in thee shall all families of the earth be blessed."

These promises should be pondered carefully. While the promise was to widen out later to include the seed of Abraham, at this stage it is purely personal. It was made to Abraham alone. He was the only representative of the race that was to be. He was an old man of seventy-five and on all human grounds it seemed utterly impossible that he should be the founder of a great race, for he was childless. But in the language of St. Paul, "He staggered not at the promise of God through unbelief: but was strong in faith" (*Romans* 4:20).

In anticipation of the geographical needs of the coming race, God gave to Abraham an inheritance in land. "For all the land which thou seest, to thee will I give it, and to thy seed for ever" (*Genesis* 3:15). "I will give it all to you and to your descendants for all time" (Moffatt). Here we see the promise of descendants still held out before him, but the years are passing and there is no sign of offspring. There is no more entrancing story of communion with, and confidence in, God than that of Abraham. That he believed God would fulfil His promise by granting him issue is abundantly clear, but it is equally clear that he was disturbed by the delay in fulfilment, and haunted by fears of failure.

"And Abram said, Lord God, what wilt thou give me, seeing I go childless, and the steward of my house *is* this Eliezer of Damascus?... to me Thou hast given no seed: and, lo, one born in my house is mine heir" (*Genesis* 15: 2-3).

Again Abraham was assured of a multitude of descendants (verse 5), and again "He believed in the Lord, and he counted it to him for righteousness" (verse 6).

The years were speeding on, and the fountains of life were drying up. Abraham was eighty-five and Sarah ten years younger. They were still without offspring and the possibility of multitudinous seed grew more and more remote. The language of his heart had a poignant ring. The question asked at a later date by some of his descendants fits his mood at this time. "Where is the promise of his coming?" (2 *Peter* 3: 4). It was at this stage that Sarah suggested a way to the realisation of their dreams. Since motherhood was denied to her, the desired goal might be reached by the mating of her husband and Hagar their slave. How easy it is for us to try to help God out by devices of our own! But this was not the way of God. He had not gone back on His promise nor forgotten it.

> "Who fathoms the eternal thought?
> Who talks of scheme and plan?
> The Lord is God! He needeth not
> The poor device of man."
> *Whittier.*

When Abraham was ninety-nine, God appeared again to him and renewed the promise of issue to him and Sarah (*Genesis* 17). It was at this time that their names were changed. Abram became Abraham, or many-father, because he was destined to be the father of many nations, and Sarai became Sarah, i.e. princess. Abraham was "as good as dead" (*Hebrews* 11:12), and laughed at the idea of becoming a father (*Genesis* 17:17) He besought God to allow Ishmael the son of Hagar, now a boy of thirteen, to rank as his heir, but

God was not to be deflected from His purpose. The promise of a child in their old age still stood and was again repeated. "Sarah thy wife shall bear thee a son indeed, and thou shalt call his name Isaac [laughter] and I will establish my covenant with him for an everlasting covenant, *and* with his seed after him" (*Genesis* 17:19). "My covenant will I establish with Isaac, which Sarah, shall bear unto thee at this set time in the next year..." (verse 21).

In the following year Isaac was born. His birth cannot be accounted for on natural, or human, grounds alone. He was a miracle child, raised up by God for a special purpose.

The terms of the Covenant with Abraham provide for both material and spiritual blessings. For a full understanding of the Covenant it is necessary to study the Old Testament passages referred to above and St. Paul's interpretation of the facts as recorded in his *Epistle to the Galatians*, especially chapters 3 and 4, and chapters 4, 8 and 11 of his *Epistle to the Romans*. The material blessings include the Promised Land as shown above and the heirship of the world. "For the promise, that he should be heir of the world, was not to Abraham, or to his seed, through the law, but through the righteousness of faith" (*Romans* 4:13). St. Paul is at particular pains to stress the fact that the blessings of this Covenant are open to descendants of "our forefather Abraham," and to all others, only through the exercise of faith. The spiritual blessings cannot be enjoyed on the ground of racial descent alone. As Abraham received his blessings because of his faith, so, too, his descendants can enter into their full heritage only through faith in our Lord Jesus Christ. The acceptance of our Lord Jesus Christ as the Redeemer of Israel and the Saviour of the world puts all believers on a basis of spiritual equality (*Galatians* 3:28), but it does not abolish racial, any more than it does sex, distinction. All are heirs according to the Promise.

It should be noted that St. Paul applies the Covenant not only to Abraham, but also to his seed. This is in keeping with the record in *Genesis* 22:15-18, after Abraham had proved his willingness to sacrifice Isaac:

"And the angel of the Lord called unto Abraham out of heaven the second time, and said: By myself have I sworn, saith the Lord, for because thou hast done this thing, and hast not withheld thy son, thine only *son*: that in blessing I will bless thee, and in multiplying I will multiply thy seed as the stars of the heaven, and as the sand which is upon the seashore: and thy seed shall possess the gate of his enemies; and in thy seed shall all the nations of the earth be blessed; because thou hast obeyed my voice."

The Covenant is now applied not only to Abraham, but to his descendants as well. Moreover, the Promise is enlarged: "Thy seed shall posses the gate of his enemies." Both Dillmann and Driver[4] read this as meaning "shall conquer and possess the cities of their enemies." The Promise adumbrates a universal empire based on the seed of Abraham as its nucleus. Later scriptures foreshadow a world-wide kingdom; and the modern trend in statesmanship is to visualise an international state, in which all nations shall play their part. The weakness in recent attempts to secure international concord lies in the spirit of compromise. The mistake lies in the attempt to evolve a new kind of state made up of contributions from each contracting nation. But there can be no compromise with God. It is part of the wonderful mercy and grace of God that "whosoever will" may enter into His Kingdom, but they may enter not on their own terms, but only on His. He has laid down the terms and conditions of membership in His Kingdom. By acceptance of those terms and the fulfilment of those conditions the way is open for all nations, and all individuals, to enter in and share the blessings promised to Abraham and to his seed forever.

---

[4] Prof. August Dillmann of Berlin, (1823 – 1894). German Orientalist and biblical scholar, esp. Ethiopic manuscripts. Rev. Prof. S.R. Driver, (1846 – 1914) Hebraic scholar, sometime Regius Professor Of Hebrew at Oxford

9

WE BELIEVE IN THE NATIONAL COVENANT, or, as it is sometimes called, The Mosaic Covenant, that is, the Covenant made by God with Israel through Moses. It is first recorded in its essence in *Exodus* 19. Three months after their deliverance from Egypt Moses was called to an audience with God on the mount and was commissioned to say to the children of Israel:

> "Now therefore, if ye will obey my voice indeed, and keep my covenant, then ye shall be a peculiar treasure unto me above all people: for all the earth is mine: and ye shall be unto me a kingdom of priests, and an holy nation. These are the words which thou shalt speak unto the children of Israel. And Moses came and called for the elders of the people, and laid before their faces all the words which the Lord had commanded him. And all the people answered together, said, all that the Lord hath spoken we will do. And Moses returned the words of the people unto the Lord" (*Exodus* 19:5-8).

Here we have a description of an official state ceremony of great importance. Moses called the elders and acquainted them with the message from God. The matter was submitted to the vote of the people. "And all the people answered together:...all that the Lord hath spoken we will do." Moses was able to carry to God the unanimous vote of the people in favour, and in advance of the details, whereon God announced His intention to address the nation after the people had prepared themselves for a state function. In majestic language, the inauguration ceremony is described in the subsequent verses: "And God spoke all these words saying ..." Then follow the Ten Commandments and the Law in its fullness. In reviewing this chapter in their history some years later Moses affirms: "The Lord our God made a covenant with us in Horeb. The Lord made not his covenant with our fathers, but with us, *even* us, who *are* all of us here alive this day. The Lord talked with you face to face in the mount out of the midst of the fire [I stood between the Lord and you at that time, to show you the word of the Lord: for ye were afraid by reason of the fire, and went not up into the mount] saying..." (*Deuteronomy* 5: 2-5).

It clearly stated that this Covenant was distinct from any made with the "fathers." St. Paul observes the distinction and stresses the fact that the National Covenant does not dis-annul the Covenant made with Abraham 430 years earlier (*Galatians* 3:17), and affirms that "It [the Law] was added because of transgressions, till the seed should come to who the promise was made" (*Galatians* 3:19).

This is a conditional covenant. It is conditioned by "if" and "but." The "if" and "but" clauses are clearly and fully stated in *Leviticus* 26, which should be carefully studied. These are preceded by a statement of general principle which admits of no argument and no controversy. "Ye shall keep my Sabbaths, and reverence my sanctuary: I am the Lord" (*Leviticus* 26:2). That is a fundamental principle on which no compromise is possible. The plural form, *Sabbaths*, should be noted. It has become fashionable in some quarters to narrow this down to Sabbath Day observance, but that is unwarranted by the text. The plural is there of set purpose. It refers not only to the due observance of the Sabbath Day, but to the sabbatic principle which runs through the whole divine scheme. It is designedly incorporated in the National Covenant. The land must have its Sabbath year of rest. "Six years thou shalt sow thy fields, and six years thou shalt prune thy vineyard, and gather in the fruit thereof: but in the seventh year shall be a Sabbath of rest unto the land, a Sabbath for the Lord: thou shalt neither sow thy field, nor prune thy vineyard" (*Leviticus* 25:3-4). Anxiety about food supplies for the eighth year is allayed by the assurance that in the sixth year the land shall produce enough to last until the eighth year crops are available (*Leviticus* 25:21).

There is also the Sabbath year of release "to the end that there be no poor among you" (*Deuteronomy* 15:4: marginal reading), which Moffatt renders, "though indeed there should be no poor among you [for the Eternal your God will prosper you in the land which the Eternal your God assigns to you as your possession] provided that you are attentive to the voice of the Eternal your God." Any system of society that precipitates squalid poverty stands condemned by its results and is contrary to the divine will and purpose.

We see then that the National Covenant provides for due recognition of the sabbatic principle. There is the Sabbath Day of rest for the toiler, the sabbatic year of rest for the land, and the sabbatic year of release from the burden of debt. The sabbatic principle extends to the year of jubilee, and even to millenniums, but the above will serve to call attention to the significance of the plural, *sabbaths*.

It is sometimes said that *Deuteronomy* 28 neutralises some of the clauses of *Leviticus* 26, but *Deuteronomy* is not a substitute for *Leviticus* 26. It is supplementary. This is expressly stated in *Deuteronomy* 29:1: "These are the words of the covenant, which the Lord commanded Moses to make with the children of Israel in the land of Moab, *besides the covenant which he made with them in Horeb.*"

10

THE COVENANT PEOPLE are clearly and definitely defined in the National Covenant. They are the children of Israel, the direct descendants of Jacob. (But we must not overlook the provision made for the admission of strangers who were prepared to assume the obligations imposed on Israel (*Leviticus* 19:33-34; *Leviticus* 24:22; *Deuteronomy* 10:18; *Joshua* 8:33). The Covenant was made with the whole of Israel, and its terms relate to the whole nation, and to any sub-divisions that might arise. At this time, Israel was a united whole and comprised the twelve tribes. As yet, there was no division into Israel and Judah.

In the commission to Moses, God defines the status of Israel, its appointed function, and its expected character. Israel was to be His "peculiar treasure." That was her status.

The word *peculiar* is one of great significance and will repay careful examination. We have come to use it as meaning *strange,* or funny, but that is far removed from its primary, or original, meaning. It is derived from a Latin word meaning *private property.* Hence its primary meaning, as given in the dictionary, is *one's own.* The English word *proper*, in its original Latin sense, is a modern equivalent. *Proper,* the dictionary tells us, means *one's own.* It is derived from the Latin word *proprius,* which itself means *one's own.* Thus a proper name is the name belonging to a certain individual, and a man's property is a possession *proper* to him, i.e. it belongs to him. It is his own. He has acquired it by his own efforts, or purchased it by his own means. No other person can claim it. Israel was God's own in a sense that no other nation was. While 'All the earth is mine,' He had special claim and title to Israel. He had acquired her by His own efforts. "Ye have seen what I did to the Egyptians, and *how* I bare you on eagle's wings, and brought you to myself" (*Exodus* 19:4). This was a national experience no other nation could boast. With tireless iteration the Scriptures declare that Israel was delivered from Egypt by the hand of God by virtue of His efforts on her behalf. St. Paul writes of "Our Saviour Lord Jesus Christ; *who gave himself for us,* that he might redeem us from all iniquity, and purify unto himself a peculiar people" (*Titus* 2:14). The underlying idea is the same in both cases. God made Israel His very own by something *He* did. "...ye are not your own...For ye are bought with a price" (1 *Corinthians* 6: 19-20).

Israel's function is defined in the words *kingdom of priests* or *a dynasty of priests* if we accept Moffatt's rendering. A priest is one commissioned to officiate in sacred offices. He stands between the people and God not because he elects to do so; self-election would be an impertinence of the highest order. Unless he is authorised and commissioned by some superior authority his activities are not valid. It should be noted that a priest does not officiate between himself and God. For the proper functioning of a priesthood there must be three parties: God, the congregation (or the individual), and the priest. A priest is a go-between. Israel was to function as a *kingdom* of priests, i.e. the kingdom was to be the unit, not the individual. As an individual priest stands between God and a third party, so Israel was to stand between God and some third party. It could hardly officiate between itself and God. In the light of other Scriptures we know the third party was the world. It was to function as a channel between God's gracious supplies and the needy world. In other words, it was chosen for service. Thus at a later date, it is said of Israel, "Thou *art* my servant, O Israel... I will preserve thee, and give thee for a covenant of the people, to establish the earth" (*Isaiah* 49:3-8).

Finally, Israel was to be a holy nation. That was its expected character. It was to be a kingdom-nation. Those two words are not synonyms. They are not two separate terms to express the same idea. It is possible to be a nation without being a kingdom. The U.S.A. is a great nation, but it is not a kingdom. A kingdom implies a king and the U.S.A. has no king. It is possible to be a kingdom without being a nation in the strict meaning of the term. The primary meaning of the word *nation*, the dictionary tells us, is 'those born of the same stock'. The former Austrian Empire was a kingdom, for it had a king-Emperor, but it was nicknamed 'The ramshackle empire' because of its admixture of various races who could not be assimilated into a racial whole.

The children of Israel were born of the same stock. They were descendants of Abraham, through the miracle child, Isaac, and Jacob. They were a kingdom, for God was their king until He was rejected by them (1 *Samuel* 8:7).

Israel was to be not only a nation, but a holy nation. The word *holy* is the modern form of the Anglo-Saxon word *halig*, which means whole or perfect in the sense of having all its component parts functioning in harmony. In the question, "Wilt thou be made whole?" the word *whole* expresses the meaning of the old word *halig*. We get the word *health* from the same source. Moffatt renders it a sacred nation. They were set apart to a sacred use, and to fail in their function was to prostitute their lives. No nation was ever called to so signal an honour, nor to so responsible a mission. God could say of them on another occasion, "This people have I formed for myself; they shall shew forth my praise" (*Isaiah* 43:21).

11

IF AND BUT. In *Leviticus* 26, the "if" and "but" clauses are clearly stated. "If ye walk in my statutes and keep my commandments, and do them ..." (*Leviticus* 26:3), manifold blessings will follow. The enumerated blessings are related to life as we know it here, and not as it may be in the hereafter. They affect both the material and the spiritual life of the community: rain, produce in plenty, immunity against attack, the companionship of God. All these things are guaranteed IF.... The mind turns naturally to the words of the Master, "Seek ye first the Kingdom of God, and his righteousness; and all these things (i.e. food and raiment) shall be added unto you" (*Matthew* 6:33). "For your heavenly Father knoweth that ye have need of all these things" (*Matthew* 6:32). It is righteousness that exalteth a nation. God guarantees unbounded prosperity to His people if they will keep His Covenant.

"*But* if ye will not hearken unto me, and will not do all these commandments..." there must follow 'as night the day' the punitive clauses enumerated in verses 14-40. These include consumption (*Leviticus* 26:16), the desolation of their sanctuaries and the wasting of their cities (*Leviticus* 26:31), the desolation of the land (*Leviticus* 26:32), and the scattering of the people amongst the heathen (*Leviticus* 26:33). All this is designed for their chastisement, and to chastise, the dictionary tells us, is "to free from faults by punishment." The punitive clauses are designed, therefore, to correct the wayward nation until, like the prodigal, it comes to itself and returns to the Father.

The period of chastisement was to be SEVEN TIMES. "I will chastise you seven times for your sins" (*Leviticus*

26:28). "And yet for all that, when they be in the land of their enemies, I will not cast them away, neither will I abhor them, to destroy them utterly, and to break my covenant with them: For I am the Lord their God. But I will for their sakes remember the covenant of their ancestors" (*Leviticus* 26:44, 45). Thus we have the promise of restoration to covenant relationship when the period of chastisement is past. Whatever may be the character of the people, God will not go back on his plighted word: "for God never goes back upon his gifts and call" (*Romans* 11:29, Moffatt).

12

The expression *seven times* occurs uniformly in *Leviticus* 26:18, 21, 24 and 28 in the AV, but Moffatt varies it as follows: "Seven times more" (verse 18), "seven strokes" (verse 21), "I will strike you seven times myself" (verse 24), and "punish you seven times over for your sins" (verse 28). Some have chosen to interpret these as cumulative; but there is no warrant for this.

Seven times equals 2,520 years, or seven times 360, a time being 360 years. It is sometimes asked how this conclusion is arrived at. We believe the Scriptures should be allowed to explain themselves and the conclusion is arrived at on the basis of the following passages. First of all, there is the principle of reckoning a day for a year. "After the number of the days in which ye searched the land, even forty days, each day for a year, shall ye bear your iniquities, *even* forty years" (*Numbers* 14:34). Ezekiel was commanded to lie on his side 'each day for a year.' "For I have laid upon thee the years of their iniquity, according to the number of the days, three hundred and ninety days: ...I have appointed thee each day for a year" (*Ezekiel* 4:5-6). In *Daniel* 12:7: "the man clothed in linen" "sware by him that liveth for ever that it *shall be* for a time, times, and half," i.e. three and a half times. In the *Book of Revelation* St. John is told by the same person, "The woman fled into the wilderness, where she hath a place prepared of God, that they should feed her there a thousand two hundred *and* three score days" (*Revelation* 12:6). In verse 14 we read the woman fled into the wilderness "for a time, and times, and half a time." It follows that the expression "time, times and half a time" equals 1,260 days, i.e. forty-two months of thirty days each. The expression forty-two months is used in *Revelation* 11:2, and again in *Revelation* 13:5. But forty-two months is three and a half years, and three and a half is half of seven. On the year day basis 1,260 days becomes 1,260 years, and twice that is 2,520 years, or the seven times of prophecy. The central date of Israel's captivity (as distinct from the captivity of Judah) is 722-1, BC. Two thousand five hundred and twenty years from that date brings us to the end of the eighteenth century when Britain's phenomenal wealth and expansion began. If this does not apply to the British and allied peoples, the promise of restoration has no known fulfilment in history. This would mean that God had gone back on His word.

13

WE BELIEVE IN THE COVENANT WITH DAVID as recorded in 2 *Samuel* 7. The setting of this Covenant and the occasion of its making are of great interest to the student. The narrative shows that it came as a surprise to David and was equally unexpected by the prophet, Nathan:

> "And it came to pass, when the king sat in his house, and the Lord had given him rest round about from all his enemies; that the king said unto Nathan the prophet, see now, I dwell in an house of cedar, but the ark of God dwelleth within curtains. And Nathan said to the king, go, do all that is in thine heart; for the Lord is with thee. And it came to pass that night, that the word of the Lord came unto Nathan, saying, Go and tell my servant David, thus saith the Lord, Shalt thou build me an house for me to dwell in?" (2 *Samuel* 7 1-5).

From this we see that Nathan approved of David's plan to build a house for the Lord, but he was divinely directed to act contrary to his own judgement. His personal judgement favoured the intention of the king, yet by divine command he had to inform David that his desire, good as that desire was, could not be carried into effect because God disapproved.

This incident casts valuable light on the larger question of Prophecy. It is often said that prophetic utterances were only expressions of the prophet's views. It is contended that Hebrew prophets were idealists who urged the people to aim at the ideals they themselves conceived, that is, they were men of the better kind who sought to realise in the life of the community their own visions of a nobler order of things. In other words, it was not an external voice that they heard but simply the uprising of their own inward thoughts. But this incident shows that such a view is untenable. The prophet was commanded to deliver a message which was the very opposite of what his own judgement approved. The message delivered by Nathan was not the outcome of his own thoughts; it was what God instructed him to deliver to the king, and was opposed to what David had proposed and what the prophet had endorsed. It does not fall within the scope of this article to discuss the question: Was the divine voice audible to the outward ear? It is enough to note that from a source not within himself the prophet received a message which ran counter to his own judgement.

We see also that David was thwarted in his desire, even thought his desire was honourable and worthy. He wished to build a house for the Lord God. "And he set masons to hew wrought stones to build the house of God, and David prepared iron in abundance...brass in abundance without weight: also cedar trees in abundance:...and David said...the house *that is* to be builded for the Lord *must be* exceeding magnifical, of fame and of glory, throughout all countries: I will therefore make preparation for it" (1 *Chronicles* 22: 2-5). David's own house was built of cedar, but the ark of God was housed in nothing more substantial than curtains. He could not reconcile this with his sense of the fitness of things, hence he desired to build a house of God which should be 'exceeding magnifical'. But he was to be balked in his design. Solomon reports, "The Lord said unto David my father: Whereas it was in thine heart to build an house unto my name, thou didst well that it was in thine heart. Nevertheless thou shalt not build the house" (1 *Kings* 8:18-19). David himself states not only the inhibition but the reason as well. "David said to Solomon: My son, as for me, it was in my mind to build an house unto the name of the Lord my God: but the word of the Lord came to me saying: thou hast shed blood abundantly, and hast made great wars: thou shalt not build an house unto my name, because thou hast shed much blood upon the earth in my sight" (1 *Chronicles* 22:6-8). David had to face what must have been a bitter disappointment to him. Some of God's choicest gifts lie in our disappointments.

There is a beautiful play upon words in this narrative, one of those touches of humour which light up so many passages of Scripture. Reduced to the simplest terms, God's message is this: "You shall not build Me a house, David, but I will build you a house." David's aim was to build a House of God, a place for sacrifice, prayer, and worship: God undertook to build for David a house in the sense of an enduring dynasty. "Thine house and thy kingdom shall be established for ever before thee: thy throne shall be established for ever" (2 *Samuel* 7:16). No such thought had been in David's mind. He had made no such request. No such prayer, as far as we know, had crossed his lips. It was both unsought and unexpected and was due entirely to the goodness and grace of God. "What can David say more unto thee? For thou, Lord God, knowest thy servant. For thy word's sake, and according to thine own heart, hast thou done all these things, to make thy servant know them" (2 *Samuel* 7 20-21).

Side by side with the narrative in the chapter before us should be read *Psalm* 89, and *Jeremiah* 33. The three-fold cord is very strong. The terms of the covenant are clear and emphatic. In the plainest of language they declare that David's throne is to endure for ever. This claim of durability is based not upon some isolated and incidental statement; it is established by the frequency of the term *for ever*. In 2 *Samuel* 7, the phrase *for ever* occurs six times. It is repeated several times in *Psalm* 89. In *Jeremiah* 33 the durability of the throne is stressed in the most emphatic language it is possible to conceive. Without giving all the passages bearing upon the everlasting nature of David's throne, the following will suffice and may be taken as typical of many others:

> "Thine house and thy kingdom shall be established for ever before thee, thy throne shall be established for ever" (2 *Samuel* 7:16).

> "His seed also will I make to endure for ever, and his throne as the days of heaven" (*Psalm* 89:29).

> "I will not lie unto David. His seed shall endure for ever, and his throne as the sun before me" (*Psalm* 35:36).

> "Thus saith the Lord; David shall never want a man to sit upon the throne of the house of Israel.... If ye can break my covenant of the day, and my covenant of the night ... *then* may also my covenant be broken with David my servant, that he should not have a son to reign upon his throne" (*Jeremiah* 33:17, 20, 21).

Unless language has ceased to have any meaning at all, these declarations mean that the throne of David is destined to last for all time.

The covenant stated in *Samuel* is amplified in *Psalm* 89. There we learn it was not merely a promise but a declaration on oath. "I have sworn unto David my servant" (verse 3). "Once have I sworn in my holiness that I will not lie unto David" (verse 35). As God swore on oath in solemn ratification of His covenant with Abraham and his seed, so also He swore to David concerning his throne. *(See section 6.)* Further, God declares He will make David "higher than the kings of the earth" (verse 27), that his enemies shall not prevail against him (verse 23), and that his power shall be on both the rivers and the sea (verse 25).

The closing verses of the Psalm complain of what seems to be a non-fulfilment of the Covenant. Incidentally, this shows that the Covenant had been regarded as a contract binding on God, and that God had entered into certain undertakings which related to the life of the monarch and the people. There came a day when these solemn asseverations seemed denied by untoward events. But whatever the author of the Psalm may have felt, to the end of his days David rejoiced in this everlasting Covenant. "These *be* the last words of David. David the son of Jesse said....The God of Israel said ... he that ruleth over men *must be* just, ruling in the fear of God ... although my house *be* not so with God; yet hath he made with me an everlasting covenant, ordered in all things, and *sure*" (2 *Samuel* 23:1-5). Though failure had to be recorded against the occupant of the throne, the Covenant remained intact and sure. Failure on the part of the king could not invalidate the Covenant.

15

This is AN UNCONDITIONAL COVENANT. There are no stipulations as to what would, or what would not, lead to its cancellation. As in the Covenant with Abraham there are no "ifs," and no "buts." There are no circumstances specified which would render the Covenant null and void. Nor does the continuance of the throne depend upon the worthiness of its occupant. The opposite is expressly stated. It was clearly foreseen that Solomon and others would prove unworthy, but their sin would in no sense abrogate the promise of continuity. "If he commit iniquity, I will chasten him with the rod of men, and with the stripes of the children of men: but my mercy shall not depart away from him, as I took it from Saul, whom I put away before thee" (2 *Samuel* 7:14-15). "If his [David's] children forsake my law, and walk not in my judgements: if they break my statutes, and keep not my commandments; then will I visit their transgression with the rod, and their iniquity with stripes. Nevertheless my loving kindness will I not utterly take from him, nor suffer my faithfulness to fail. My covenant will I not break nor alter the thing that is gone out of my lips" (*Psalm* 89:30-35). The durability of the throne is not dependent upon any qualities of the monarch, inherent or acquired. It is guaranteed by God without any specified conditions expressed or implied.

Interwoven with the Covenant relating to the throne of David is a solemn declaration in regards to the Israel people and their future home.

"Moreover I will appoint a place for my people Israel, and will plant them, and they shall dwell in a place of their own, and move no more: neither shall the children of wickedness afflict them any more, as beforetime" (2 *Samuel* 7: 10).

From a strictly literary point of view this seems like an interjection without any relation to the subject of the narrative; but that only serves to increase its significance. David was the king of Israel, and God assures him that both the throne and the people shall endure for ever. "For thou hast confirmed to thyself thy people Israel *to be* a people unto thee for ever: and thou, Lord, art become their God" (2 *Samuel* 7:24). A throne without a state is as unthinkable as a king without a kingdom. The throne of David was the throne of Israel. It is a logical necessity that if the throne abides the people should continue. In biblical times, no less than in modern times, there have been those who have proclaimed the cessation of Israel. "Considerest thou not what this people have spoken, saying, the two families which the Lord hath chosen, he hath even cast them off....If my covenant be not with day and night....Then will I cast away the seed of Jacob, and David my servant, so that I will not take any of his seed to be rulers over the seed of Abraham, Isaac, and Jacob" (*Jeremiah* 33:24-26). "If those ordinances depart from before me ... the seed of Israel also shall cease from being a nation before me for ever"(*Jeremiah* 31:36). Here we see that God protests against the assumption that He has cast away His people. St. Paul contested the same idea. "Hath God cast away His people? God forbid ... God hath not cast away his people which he foreknew" (*Romans* 11:1-2). Over and over again God declares that Israel shall abide for ever. "For as the new heavens and the new earth, which I will make, shall remain before me, saith the Lord, so shall your seed and your name remain" (*Isaiah* 66:22). Against this there can be no appeal. The mouth of the Lord hath spoken it. It follows that Israel must be in existence still.

It is distinctly stated that God would appoint a place where Israel would be planted, a place from which they should move no more, and which should not be invaded by the enemy. It is sometimes said the appointed place was Palestine, but the Holy Land in no way meets the requirements of the text. The tense of the verb is against it in the first place. Israel was actually in Palestine at this time, but God's promise is in the future tense. It was something yet to be. In the second place, Israel was forcibly removed from Palestine by her enemies. The land was invaded by enemy kings and a succession of deportations scattered Israel for and wide. Tiglath-Pileser (745-727 BC) Shalmaneser V (727-722 BC), Sargon II (722-705 BC), Sennacherib (705-681 BC), Esarhaddon (680-669 BC) Nebuchadnezzar (604-561 BC), each in turn uprooted the Israel people from the Holy Land and scattered them among the surrounding nations. Unless God has broken His promise, the appointed place must be some other land than Palestine. Isaiah addresses

Israel in the isles. "Listen, O isles, unto me; and hearken, ye people, from afar…. Thou art my servant, O Israel, in whom I will be glorified" (*Isaiah* 49:1-3). The only isles that meet the requirements are the British Isles. Jews still use Isaiah's Hebrew phrase to describe the British Isles. The Chief Rabbi of South Africa, Prof. Dr. J. L. Landau, writes me: "It is quite correct that the phrase 'Isles of the Sea' is often applied to Great Britain, in fact, I myself used that phrase in a poem dealing with Great Britain." These islands have never been invaded by a foreign foe since the Normans landed in the eleventh century, and these we believe to be the main body of the tribe of Benjamin moving to the appointed place where they have become securely planted.

Several volumes are available in which the wanderings of Israel are traced to their arrival at 'the appointed place.[5] It will be sufficient for the purposes of this little book to mention important links in the chain of evidence. Josephus records the deportation of ten-tribed Israel by Shalmaneser to Media and Persia,[6] and 2 *Esdras* 13:45, leaves them at Arsareth after their adventurous crossing of the Euphrates.

The opening paragraph of the *Anglo-Saxon Chronicle*[7] says:

> "The first inhabitants were the Britons, who came from Armenia, and first peopled Britain southward. Then happened it, that the Picts came south from Scythia, with long ships, not many; and, landing first in the northern part of Ireland, they told the Scots that they must dwell there. But they would not give them leave; for the Scots told them that they could not all dwell there together; "But," said the Scots, "we can nevertheless give you advice. We know another island here to the east. There you may dwell, if you will; and whosoever withstandeth you, we will assist you, that

---

[5] For more information the reader is referred to (amongst others) *The Message of The Minor Prophets* Rev. A.F. Rash (CP19); *God's Great Plan* R. Llewelyn Williams (CP12); *Celt Druid and Culdee* I. Hill-Elder (CP02): available from The Covenant Publishing Company Ltd. www.covpub.co.uk

[6] *Antiquities Of The Jews*, Flavius Josephus. Book 9, Chapter 14, paragraph 1.

[7] *Anglo-Saxon Chronicles* translated by Rev. James Ingram 1823 Everyman Edition.

you may gain it." Then went the Picts and entered this land northward. Southward the Britons possessed it, as we before said. And the Picts obtained wives of the Scots, on condition that they chose their kings always on the female side; which they have continued to do, so long since. And it happened, in the run of years, that some party of Scots went from Ireland into Britain, and acquired some portion of this land. Their leader was called Reoda, from whom they are named Dalreodi (or Dalreathians)".

The substance of the above is embodied in the first chapter of *The Ecclesiastical History of England*, by Bede, (c. AD 673-735). [8] If we accept the evidence of an ancient manuscript, St. Columba was divinely commissioned to ordain Aidan King of Dalriada (AD 574-604).[9]

The Scottish Declaration of Independence now in the Register House in Edinburgh, and described by the Register House officials as "Probably our most precious possession," supports the *Anglo-Saxon Chronicle* in important details. "The Scottish Declaration of Independence" was "drawn up by Bernard de Linton, Abbot of Aberbrothock and Chancellor of Scotland, and sent to Pope John XXII by Scottish Estates in Parliament, Assembled in the Abbey of Aberbrothock under the presidency of King Robert the Bruce, on 6th April, AD 1320". This precious document says, *inter alia*, "We know, Most Holy Father and Lord, and from the chronicles and books of the ancients gather, that among other illustrious nations, ours, to wit the nation of the Scots, has been distinguished by many honours; which passing from the greater Scythia through the Mediterranean Sea and Pillars of Hercules and sojourning in Spain among the most savage tribes through a long course of time, could nowhere be subjugated by any people however barbarous; and coming thence one thousand two hundred years after the outgoing of the people of Israel, they, by many victories and infinite toil,

---

[8] *A History Of The English Church and People (The Ecclesiastical History of England)* Bede Trans. L. Sherley-Price (Penguin) 1965
[9] *"Life of St. Columba"* St. Adamnan, 9th Abbot of Iona (7th Century)

acquired for themselves possessions in the West which they now hold.... In their kingdom one hundred and thirteen kings of their own royal stock, no stranger intervening, have reigned...."

The Prayer Book of Queen Victoria's time contained the following collect for June 20th (*The Queen's Accession*): "Let there never be wanting in her house to succeed her in the government of this United Kingdom, that our posterity may see her children's children, and peace upon Israel, so that we thy people and sheep of thy pasture, shall give thee thanks for ever."

From these excerpts it is abundantly clear that the people of England and Scotland assumed their Israel descent, and looked to the very place where the ten-tribed Israel was lost as their ancient home.

"Once have I sworn by my holiness that I will not lie unto David. His seed shall endure for ever, and his throne as the sun before me" (*Psalm* 89:35-36). As was pointed out in section 1, the first article in The Faith of a British Israelite is: We believe God. We believe God made this far-reaching promise, and we believe He has so fulfilled His promise, that there has never been lacking a descendant of David to occupy the enduring throne. It follows that that throne must be in existence still, and that a descendant of David occupies that throne, or God has lied. In another place[10] I have examined briefly the history of every known kingdom in the world in an endeavour to find a throne that meets the requirements of this Covenant. There is only one such throne in the world, but there is one. It is the throne of Britain. On various occasions I have examined the Royal Chart in the Royal Library, Windsor Castle. That Chart shows the descent of The British Monarchy from Adam.

---

[10] *The Kingdom of God on Earth* Rev. Alban Heath (The Covenant Publishing Company Ltd, 1933)

WE BELIEVE IN THE *NEW COVENANT IN CHRIST JESUS.*

> "Behold, the days come, saith the Lord, that I will make a new covenant with the House of Judah; not according to the covenant that I made with their fathers in the day that I took them by the hand to bring them out of the land of Egypt: which my covenant they brake, although I was an husband unto them, saith the Lord: but this *shall be* the covenant that I will make with the House of Israel: after those days, saith the Lord, I will put my law in their inward parts, and write it in their hearts: and will be their God, and they shall be my people. And they shall teach no more every man his neighbour and every man his brother, saying: Know the Lord: for they shall all know me from the least of them unto the greatest of them, saith the Lord, for I will forgive their iniquity, and I will remember their sin no more" (*Jeremiah* 31: 31-34).

This is repeated in *Hebrews* 8:8-12. It will be noted that this is set in contrast with the Mosaic Covenant in which the law was written on tables of stone. Those were breakable, but the law written in the heart must go wherever man himself goes and abide as long as Israel abides.

That this new Covenant is associated with our Lord Jesus Christ may be inferred from the forgiveness of sin; but other Scriptures make it abundantly plain that the new Covenant comes with and through Jesus Christ. "The word of the Lord to Israel by Malachi" (*Malachi*.1:1) declares: "Behold, I will send my messenger, and he shall prepare the way before me: and the Lord, whom ye seek, shall suddenly come to his temple, even the messenger of the covenant, whom ye delight in; behold, he shall come, saith the Lord of hosts" (*Malachi* 3: 1). John the Baptist announced himself as "A voice crying in the wilderness, Prepare ye the way of the Lord," and at the institution of the Lord's Supper our Lord said, "Drink ye all of it: for this is my blood of the New Testament [covenant] which is shed for many for the remission of sins" (*Matthew* 26: 28).

It will be noted that there is a national and an individual aspect of this. It is a Covenant with the House of Israel, and with the House of Judah; but forgiveness of sin is a personal matter, and that is obtained through the 'covenant-blood' of Christ, to use, Moffatt's phrase.

17

Forgiveness of sin remains an unfathomable mystery to the human mind. "It may be that God can forgive sins, but I don't see how he can," said Socrates long ago. We have not advanced far beyond that. We know he does forgive, but *how* remains a mystery. Though the wonder and mystery of forgiveness may baffle the understanding we still cry with the Psalmist: "There is forgiveness with thee," and the experience of forgiveness is one to which millions can testify. All that may be said against empiricism will not alter the fact one iota. The millions who have experienced forgiveness maintain the attitude of the blind man who had recovered his sight. In current speech, his answer to those who doubted the reality of the miracle was this: "All that you say about the scientific impossibility of a man once blind being made to see makes not a shade of difference to me. One thing I know: I was blind, now I can see. Explain it if you can; deny it if you will. I know I can see. The experience is enough to satisfy me." The millions who have experienced God's healing forgiveness know they have peace with God through our Lord Jesus Christ whatever scientific barriers may seen to lie in the way of its achievement. Experience satisfies them of its reality. They are humbled by the wonder of it.

18

While we may not be able to explain the mystery, it is profitable to dwell upon it, for the wonder of it grows upon us as we reflect upon the theme. The Atonement may baffle human understanding, but to discard it because we cannot explain it would be silly. The word Atonement is good, plain English and bears its meaning upon its face. It is simply at-one-ment where "one" retains its original sound as in "only." Shakespeare uses the verb form transitively in "I did atone my countryman and thee,"[11] that is, 'I bridged the gulf between you, I brought you together again, I reconciled you'. So, "God was in Christ reconciling the world unto himself" (2 *Corinthians* 5:19). In other words, God through Christ restores the human soul to its harmonious relationship with Himself.

From our Lord's own words quoted above we see that Atonement is effected through the shedding of His blood. 'The blood is the life.'[12] By His own voluntary act, He gave His life a ransom for many. "I lay down my life of myself. I have power to lay it down, and I have power to take it again" (*John* 10:18). The shedding of His blood must not be restricted to the discharge of blood consequent on His being nailed to the Cross. Very little blood issued from the palms and insteps. Jesus did not die as a result of crucifixion. Victims of that barbarous act lingered for some days and usually died from physical exhaustion. But the narrative of the Crucifixion makes it clear that Jesus died from some other cause. That cause is explained in *John* 19:34: "One of the soldiers with a spear pierced his side, and forthwith came there out blood and water." Great medical authorities like Simpson,[13] the discoverer of chloroform, have declared that

---

[11] *Cymbeline* 4:i William Shakespeare

[12] *Leviticus* 17:11 "For the life of the flesh *is* in the blood: and I have given it to you upon the altar to make an atonement for your souls: for it *is* the blood *that* maketh an atonement for the soul."

[13] "The effect of that wounding or piercing of the side was an escape of 'blood and water,' visible to the apostle John standing some distance off; and I do not believe that anything could possibly account for this appearance, as described by that apostle, except a collection of blood effused into the distended sac of the pericardium in consequence of rupture of the heart, and afterwards separated, as is usual with extravasated blood, into those two parts, viz. (1) crassamentum or red

the mixture of blood and water indicates a fractured pericardium, or a broken heart, and there would follow the complete draining of blood from his body. After His resurrection, Jesus challenged His disciples to "Handle me and see; for a spirit hath not flesh and bones as ye see me have" (*Luke* 24:39). There is no reference to blood. That had been drained away, and with it had gone his life.

As I have said above, this was a voluntary act on the part of our Lord. "The Son of man came... to give his life a ransom *for many*" (*Matthew* 20: 28). It had been prophesied of the expected Messiah, "He shall confirm the covenant *with many* for one week" (*Daniel* 9: 27). At the institution of the Lord's Supper our Lord said: "This is my blood of the new covenant, which is shed for many for the remission of sins" (*Matthew* 26: 28). The recurrence of the phrase *for many* cannot be accidental. It links the component parts of the chain. If we ask what caused that cardiac rupture which precipitated His death, the Scriptures supply the answer: "Reproach hath broken my heart and I am full of heaviness: and I looked for some to take pity, but there was none; and for comforters, but I found none" (*Psalm* 69:20). That experience befell Him on the Cross when He cried, "My God, why hast thou forsaken me?" The Divine presence was eclipsed and He passed into outer darkness. The intensity of that extreme experience is shown by its result. His heart was broken.

Along these lines we can trace the physical experience connected with the Atonement, but after that we are beyond our depth. We are carried into regions where human intelligence fails us. He came to give His life a ransom for many. A ransom, the dictionary tells us, is a "price paid for redemption from captivity or punishment." To whom was the price paid? "Ye are not your own; ye are bought with a price." From what are we bought? To whom is the price paid? Here the light of reason fails us.

---

clot, and (2) watery serum." *Sir J. Y. Simpson, M.D., etc,* quoted in *Our Lord's Life on Earth* by the Rev. Prof. William Hanna, DD., (Robert Carter, 1869) p.652

"We have but faith. We cannot know,
For knowledge is of things we see."[14]

Like the blind man, we fall back on experience. "We know
that we have passed from death to life because...."[15] An inner
voice breathes its benediction of peace and we are at rest.

19

From this sacrifice of the Son of God certain things
result. There is redemption for Israel and salvation available
for the whole world. Salvation and redemption are not
interchangeable terms. They stand for two separate acts. In
Hebrew, in Greek, and in English the distinction is clear: "I
the Lord am thy Saviour (*yasha*) and thy Redeemer (*gaal*)"
(*Isaiah* 60:16). The Hebrew word for Saviour means to save,
or to give ease, while the Hebrew word for Redeemer means
to set free by avenging, or repaying.
"Blessed *be* the Lord God of Israel; for he hath visited
and Redeemed (*lutroo*) his people, and hath raised up an horn
of Salvation (*soteria*) for us in the house of his servant
David" (*Luke* 1:68). (*Lutroo* means to make loose by a
price, and *soteria* means to save, or bring safe out of evil.)
"Christ hath Redeemed us from the curse of the law... that
the blessing of Abraham might come on the Gentiles through
Jesus Christ" (*Galatians* 3:14). To redeem, the dictionary
tells us, is 'to ransom: to relieve from captivity by a price.'
As a result of Christ's vicarious and atoning death, Israel is
relieved from captivity, and every individual, whether of
Israel or of any other race or people, may be brought safe out
of evil. "He shall save his people from their sins."[16] "There
is none other name under heaven given among men, whereby
we must be saved" (*Acts* 4: 12).

---

[14] *In Memoriam* Alfred, Lord Tennyson
[15] 1*John* 3:14 "We know that we have passed from death unto life, because we love the brethren.
He that loveth not *his* brother abideth in death."
[16] *Matthew* 1:21 "And she shall bring forth a son, and thou shalt call his name Jesus: for he shall
save his people from their sins."

THE ONE SEED WHICH IS CHRIST. Some stumble over the words of St. Paul in *Galatians* 3:16, thinking that Christ has abolished all that went before, but the very opposite is St. Paul's argument. He contends that the Law does not abolish the Promise made centuries before the Law was given. The New Covenant in Christ Jesus is the most important of all. It is the coping-stone of the whole structure of Promise and Covenant inasmuch as it makes all the Promises doubly sure. "For all the promises of God in him *are* yea, and in him Amen," (2 *Corinthians* 1:20), or, as Moffatt renders the passage, "The divine 'yes' has at last sounded in him, for in him is the 'yes' that affirms all the promises of God." Again St. Paul declares, "Jesus Christ was a minister of the circumcision for the truth of God, to confirm the promises *made* unto the fathers" (*Romans* 15:8), or, in Moffatt's words, "Christ, I mean, became a servant to the circumcised in order to prove God's honesty by fulfilling His promises to the fathers." Not only are the covenant blessings guaranteed by God on oath; they are made legally certain by the testament in the blood of Christ.

It is profitable to mark the meticulous accuracy of Biblical writers in the use of technical terms. Our Lord speaks of the new testament in His blood. A wonderful passage in *Hebrews* 9 compares the efficacy of the blood of bulls and goats with the blood of Christ, and proceeds, "And for this cause he is the mediator of the new testament, that by means of death... they which are called might receive the promise of eternal inheritance. For where a testament *is*, there must also of necessity be the death of the testator. For a testament *is* of force after men are dead: otherwise it is of no strength at all while the testator liveth" (verses 15-17).

The writer is calling attention to the distinction between a will and a testament. We speak of "The last will and testament of...." As long as the testator lives, the document is nothing more than a will. It sets forth the present intention, or desire, of the testator, but as long as he lives it is possible to alter, or cancel, all its terms. His death transforms the will into a testament. It can no longer be altered except by costly and difficult legal processes. The death of Christ has confirmed the promises of God and translated the covenants into a legal document. This distinction is brought out in Moffatt's translation, which reads: "He mediates a new covenant for this reason, that those who have been called may obtain the eternal inheritance they have been promised.... Thus, in case of a will, the death of the testator must be announced. A will only holds in cases of death; it is never valid so long as the testator is alive." Therefore, all the promises of God are confirmed by the death of Christ and may be claimed by the legal heirs. By his vicarious faith, Abraham brought his descendants into covenant relation with God. "Because thou hast done this thing... in thy seed shall all the nations of the earth be blessed; because thou hast obeyed my voice" (*Genesis* 22:16-18). Abraham was made 'heir of the world' not through the law but through the righteousness of faith (*Romans* 4:13). Christ has confirmed all the promises made to the fathers and opened the Kingdom of Heaven to all believers, making it possible for whosoever will to become "Abraham's seed" and heirs according to the promise (*Galatians* 3:29). By faith in our Lord Jesus Christ the way into Abraham's inheritance is open "That the blessing of Abraham might come on the Gentiles through Jesus Christ: that we might receive the promise of the Spirit through faith" (*Galatians* 3:14). By his vicarious faith Abraham bequeathed a blessing to a race; by His vicarious death Christ has not only confirmed the promises made unto the fathers, but made unmeasured blessing available to whosoever will. The Covenant with Abraham was unconditional; the new Covenant in Christ Jesus is conditional. We can obtain the promised blessings only *if* we have faith.

In keeping with Biblical teaching, WE BELIEVE THAT ISRAEL AND JUDAH, WERE, AND ARE, SEPARATE AND DISTINCT ENTITIES. Failure to recognise this elementary distinction accounts for much of the confused thought that exists. We affirm that much of the Bible cannot be understood until this distinction is recognised. It is a common experience for our workers, when speaking to the British about British-Israel, to be met with the remark, "I'm not a Jew." It seems to be assumed that to say the British are Israel is tantamount to saying they are Jews. Nothing could be farther from the truth. We venture to say that were such looseness in the use of terms as prevails in Biblical discussion common in other branches of learning there would be utter confusion. The laxity which is condoned in this department would not be tolerated in any other sphere. It is not uncommon to find Abraham described as a Jew. Even Milman in his standard work, *The History of the Jews*, lapses into this error and even the highly respected late Bishop Ryle of Liverpool (while condemning the tendency to give Biblical terms a meaning they cannot bear) writes of "the whole Jewish or Twelve-tribed nation."[17] We affirm in the most categorical terms that neither Abraham, nor Isaac, nor Jacob was a Jew. They were Hebrews. All the ancient Israelites were Hebrews. The term Jew as a national appellation does not appear until some fourteen hundred years after Abraham.

22

There are three uses of the term *Israel* in the Bible, and no other. As a result of his spiritual crisis when he faced the angel alone, Jacob's name was changed from Jacob to Israel. "Thy name shall be called no more Jacob, but Israel" (*Genesis* 32:28). Israel became his personal, God-given name. As a natural consequence, his descendants became the

---

[17] *Coming Events and Present Duties.* Bishop J. C. Ryle (London, 1879)

children of Israel, or Israelites. The third use of the name is connected with the rebellious ten-tribed kingdom. At the disruption of the kingdom after Solomon's death, the separatists assumed the racial name, Israel. It may have been in arrogance or defiance, but whatever the explanation the fact remains that they did. Consequently, as any Bible atlas will show, there emerged the kingdom of Israel and the kingdom of Judah. "So when all Israel saw that the king hearkened not unto them, the people answered the king, saying, what portion have we in David? Neither have we inheritance in the son of Jesse: to your tents, O Israel; now see to thine own house, David. So Israel departed unto their tents" (1 *Kings* 12:16). "I can only discover three senses in which the word Israel is used," wrote Bishop Ryle,[18] and the three senses are those given above. The claim made by Doctor H.L. Goudge[19] and others that the Church is the new Israel has no Biblical authority for it. As Bishop Ryle wrote: "Where in the whole of the New Testament shall we find any plain authority for applying the word Israel to anyone but the Nation Israel? I can find none."[20]

The term *Jew* as a national name does not appear until the last half of the sixth century BC. Josephus, the Jewish historian, informs us that the Babylonian exiles who returned to Jerusalem under the Edict of Cyrus *c*. 536 BC adopted, or were known by, that name.[21] There is an earlier use of the term in 2 *Kings* 16:6, but not as a national appellation. Ahaz complained to Tiglath-Pileser that the king of Syria had invaded Elath, one of his most distant provinces at the head of the Gulf of Akabah, and had driven out some Jews. But Ahaz was styled king of Judah both before and after that episode. The term *Jew* is derived from Judah, one of the twelve sons of Jacob.[22] To say that Abraham was a Jew is

---

[18] ibid.

[19] Canon H.L. Goudge (1866-1939)

[20] op.cit. *Coming Events and Present Duties*

[21] "So the Jews prepared for the work: that is the name they are called by from the day that they came up from Babylon, which is taken from the tribe of Judah, which came first to these places, and thence both they and the country gained that appellation." op.cit *Antiquities Of The Jews.* Book 11, Ch.5, para. 7.)

[22] [f. OF *giu* f. L f. Gk *Ioudaios* f. Aramaic *y'hudai*=Heb. *y'hudi* f. *y'hudah* Judah] *The Concise Oxford Dictionary* (1949)

worse than saying a man is his own grandchild. No one would dream of saying the Afrikaners are Hollanders, or that Australians are Englishmen. Afrikaners in part are descendants of the people of Holland. In no sense can they be called, nor would they claim to be, Hollanders. They are an offshoot of the parent body. In the same way, the Jews are an offshoot of the parent body, the parent body being Israel.

23

Both in history and in prophecy the distinction between Israel and Judah is commonly recognised, as the following examples will show:

> "The children of Israel were 300,000 and the men of Judah 30,000" (1 *Samuel* 11:8).
> "I will sow the house of Israel and the house of Judah with the seed of man" (*Jeremiah* 31:27).
> "I will make a new covenant with the house of Israel, and with the house of Judah" (*Jeremiah* 31: 31).
> "It shall come to pass... that the house of Judah shall walk to the house of Israel" (*Jeremiah* 3:18: Margin).
> "The elders of Judah came and sat before me" (*Ezekiel* 8:1).
> "Then came certain of the elders of Israel unto me" (*Ezekiel* 14:1).

These are but a few of the many scriptures which treat the two peoples as separate.[23] It may be objected that St. Paul claimed to be both a Jew and also an Israelite and that therefore the two terms are inter-changeable. But this is to ignore the meticulous accuracy of the Scriptures and to overlook the fact that St. Paul was a master dialectician. In the mêlée at Jerusalem "The Jews... stirred up all the people, and laid hands on Paul" (*Acts* 21:27), but demanding to be

---

[23] Our Lord was in ceaseless conflict with the Jews, but He sent His disciples on a kindly mission to "the lost sheep of the house of Israel." (*Matthew* 10:6)

heard, he exclaimed: "I am a man *which am* a Jew" (verse 39). It was a diplomatic move and showed his astuteness. In writing to the Romans he says, "I also am an Israelite, of the seed of Abraham, of the tribe of Benjamin" (*Romans* 11:1). Both statements are strictly true. When the kingdom was rent, God declared his purpose of giving the tribe of Benjamin to the southern kingdom of Judah as a light to David and his sons for ever (1 *Kings* 11:36, and 12:23). These, it appears, remained with Judah until their flight prior to the fall of Jerusalem in A.D. 70, when they left in terms of the prophecy of *Jeremiah* 6:1. I think it was the late Dean Farrar[24] who expressed the view that all the twelve disciples except Judas were of the tribe of Benjamin. As the tribe of Benjamin remained an integral part of Judah, St. Paul was entitled to call himself a Jew, just as a South African domiciled in the Transvaal is entitled to call himself a Transvaaler, or a man of Kent to call himself an Englishman.

24

Jeremiah refers to "The two families which the Lord hath chosen," and declares their survival is as sure as the sun and moon (*Jeremiah* 33: 24-25). Each family has its separate function in the nation, "Judah was his sanctuary, and Israel his dominion" (*Psalms* 114:2). "... [Reuben's] birthright was given unto the sons of Joseph... Of [Judah] came the chief ruler; but the birthright was Joseph's" (1 *Chronicles* 5:1-2). Had the rule of primogeniture been followed, Reuben, Jacob's first born, should have inherited the birthright, but because he had disgraced himself it was taken from him and given to Joseph (See also *Genesis* 49:3-4). While not the ruling tribe, Judah was to supply the chief ruler (*Genesis* 49:10), and to the Jews were committed the oracles of God. (*Romans* 3:2). That Judah fulfilled both these functions can be amply demonstrated. During the long, dark days while Israel was lost Judah preserved the sacred records, and

---

[24] Dean F.W. Farrar of Canterbury, (1831 – 1903).

authoritative charts show that Queen Elizabeth II is descended from David of Judah.[25] The final rule will be that of our Lord, Who was addressed as, and accepted the title of, "Son of David." Moreover, the word of the Lord still stands: "The Lord God shall give unto him the throne of his father David: and he shall reign over the house of Jacob for ever: and of his kingdom there shall be no end" (*Luke* 1:32-33).

The function of Israel was to exercise government, "Israel was his dominion." "The birthright was given unto the sons of Joseph" (1 *Chronicles* 5:1), .i.e. Ephraim and Manasseh. Manasseh was to grow into a great people, and Ephraim was to become a multitude of nations (*Genesis* 48:19). These two promises are clearly fulfilled in the British Commonwealth, and the United States of America. The U.S.A. is officially a "people." In the courts of justice it is 'The People *v.* so-and-so.' We know they are a great people. The British Commonwealth is a nation and a company of nations (*Genesis* 35:11). The prophecy finds its fulfilment in these two peoples as in no other. The record of their success in government, particularly that of the Commonwealth, is written large across the pages of history.

> "Of all the countries in this Europe of ours, which has done so much in the way of exploring and populating the earth, it is Great Britain whose colonising instinct has contributed most toward giving it form and life.... What would the world be without the British Empire?.... We have to see how Great Britain added to her possessions from generation to generation, and ended by assembling beneath her flag the largest, the richest, and the most populous empire the world has ever seen."[26]

---

[25] See book and chart *The Royal House of Britain: An Enduring Dynasty* by the Rev. W. M. H. Milner, MA (CP36) *15ᵗʰ Edn.* 1991 available from The Covenant Publishing Company Ltd.
[26] *The British Empire: a study in Colonial Geography,* Albert Demangeon, Professor of Geography at the Sorbonne, (*L'Empire britannique*) 1923 pp. 12-14

Israel emerged from its period of chastisement at the end of the eighteenth century, when Britain entered upon the period of expansion referred to by the French professor in the preceding paragraph. Judah is now emerging from its own period of chastisement. Its period of decline began in 604 BC when Nebuchadnezzar reduced Judah to vassalage, and the treading down of Jerusalem by the Gentiles began (*Luke* 21:24). Seven times, or 2,520 years, after 604 BC brings us to AD 1917,[27] when Jerusalem was delivered from Gentile rule. Judah's final crash came in 586 BC when Jerusalem was sacked, the Temple destroyed, and the king deported in strict accord with prophecy (See 2 *Kings* 25, and *Ezekiel* 12:12). There was thus a period of eighteen years of undoing for Judah, from 604 BC to 586 BC. 2,520 years later this brought us to 1935, by which time reformed Israel in the west emerged as a "company of nations", being and benefiting from a "Commonwealth", in the real sense of the word, having moved on from the days of the British Empire.

The trauma of world events at this Age-end period interrupted the final restoration of Israel during the 20th century. It is also necessary to point out that the emergence of the Jewish State in Israel, in 1948, proved to be a counterfeit of the real restored Israel. The Israeli State, (a political construct; not being a nation as such), was and remains a source of mounting conflict in the Middle East. It has led to enormous prophetic confusion amongst Christians as to the identity of true Israel – that is, the vast "New Jerusalem" of the Covenant Nations centred on the Royal British Throne of the Lord. Through being under constant attack, the Israeli State has not been able, or willing, to fully comply with the requirements of the 1917 Balfour Declaration[28], which stated that 'nothing shall be done which may prejudice the civil and religious rights of existing non-Jewish communities in Palestine".

---

[27] When calculating from B.C. to A.D. dates add 1.

[28] The Balfour Declaration of 1917: letter to Lord Rothschild from Arthur James Balfour, British Foreign Secretary. (See end notes.)

World War II; the 'wind of change' that blew upon the Commonwealth from 1960; and now the European Union: all have diverted restored Israel from its destiny of leading the nations in peace and towards the fullness of the Kingdom of God upon earth. This must be seen as a temporary set-back only. The false systems of prophetic Babylon in the political, economic and religious spheres will pass away in the fullness of time, perhaps sooner than appears possible in this first decade of the 21st century.

26

WE BELIEVE IN THE COMING OF THE KINGDOM OF GOD ON EARTH.   Rabbinical authorities are quoted as saying the Hebrew Scriptures contain very little about our life after death.   The burden of their message is concerned with earthly life under the headship of the Messiah, under whose government mundane conditions will more truly reflect the will of God.   That is not to ignore the spiritual life 'when we have shuffled off this mortal coil.'   The trusting soul has no doubt about God's willingness and ability to provide for the soul, or personality, after death.   But the other world is veiled.   "Eye hath not seen, nor ear heard, neither have entered into the heart of man, the things which God hath prepared for them that love him"   (1 *Corinthians* 2:9).   The Father's gracious provision for His children after death lies beyond our comprehension.   But that it is great and glorious the Scriptures made abundantly clear.   "Beloved, now are we the sons of God, and it doth not yet appear what we shall be: but we know that when he shall appear we shall be like him: for we shall see him as he is" (1 *John* 3:2).   While we believe, and accept with reverent confidence, all the gracious promises concerning our future life, we accept with equal confidence all the promises relating to life as we know it on this earthly plane.   We believe 'The best is yet to be,' and that the best will come to pass when the Messianic Kingdom is established on the earth.

God is the only Sovereign Ruler in the Universe. "The Lord hath prepared his throne in the heavens; and his kingdom ruleth over all" (*Psalm* 103:19). Ignoring for the moment the conflict which resulted in the casting out of Satan from heaven (*Revelation.* 12:7-9), we may assume that God's will prevails in the heavens. Jesus taught us to pray, "Our Father...Thy will be done on earth, as it is done in heaven." From this we must infer two things: first that the will of God is done in heaven, second, that it is not fully done on earth. If God's will were the rule of earthly life there would be no need to pray that prayer. Man's incursions into the province of 'the only wise potentate' have disturbed the order and harmony that should prevail in human relationships and earthly life. We have substituted man-made laws for the Divine laws. This has resulted in our own undoing and in the chaos which prevails to-day. Experiments in human government were permitted by God so that we might learn the value of Divine rule, and welcome it by voluntary choice. Virtue that is forced upon us has little moral value. We have to grow to the knowledge that "It's wiser being good than bad,"[29] and, like our great Exemplar, learn obedience by the things we suffer (*Hebrews* 5:8). The bitter experiences through which the world is now passing are disposing men to seek a better social order. There is a blind groping after that constituted order of society which is revealed in the Bible as the Messianic Kingdom, or the Kingdom of God on earth. The time limit of permissive earthly rule and authority is rapidly approaching, and the Kingdom of God is nigh at hand.

27

The pendulum of human thought swings to and fro. We have had extreme individualism when the social whole has scarcely come into the purview. We have had the idea of the social whole almost ruling out the rights and privileges of the individual, as in Russian Communism, now abandoned. We

---

[29] *Apparent Failure* (Stanza 7) Robert Browning

have had the changes rung on 'The Sabbath was made for man' and 'Man was made for the Sabbath.' Professor Huxley[30] tilted against the practice of regarding man as made for technology, whereas technology should be made for man. In the religious world we have had the stress laid on man's spiritual needs almost to the exclusion of the physical environment in which he has had to live his life. We have detached the Kingdom of God from reality and related it to life above the bright blue sky, while all the time men are clamouring for a Kingdom of God on earth. Many have confessed that the idealism of the pulpit wilts and withers in the fierce light of practical realities. The aspirations induced on Sunday are dashed on the rocks on Monday. Mr. Clive Kenrick, himself a prominent business man and head of a century-old firm, and a devout and earnest Christian, says: "We agree that modern business and Christianity are incompatible."[31] In other words, the social and economic environment, over which the individual has no control, make impossible the realisation of the dreams and aspirations of the soul. We are trying to live a spiritual life in a material world which is governed by materialistic forces. While there are millions of earnest Christians in the world, the world itself, as far as its organised life is concerned, is un-Christian, and, in many respects, anti-Christian. It is like leaving a child to play in the mud with the strict injunction that she must keep her dress clean. While we must never lose sight of man's spiritual needs, we must not overlook the inimical environment in which, under the present order, he is compelled without choice to live his life. The social structure is wrong. The economic structure is wrong. The political structure is wrong. None is shaped according to the pattern shown on the Mount. The workmen have arrogated to themselves the right to disregard, or to modify, the Architect's plans and specifications, and, consequently, the whole structure is wrong. It is so wrong that it is now beyond human ingenuity to put it right. As the displacement factor in

---

[30] Professor Huxley 1825 –1895 Renowned for supporting Darwinism.
[31] *The True Economic System: The Witness Of The Economic System; The Scriptures; The Great Pyramid:* Clive Kenrick (The Covenant Publishing Company, 1933) p.35.

the Great Pyramid threw out the alignment so that the chief corner stone, or apex stone, would not fit, so society as it is organised today rules out Christ Who is "the chief Corner Stone." Only the establishment of the Kingdom of God on earth can restore order out of the existing chaos.

28

In the religious world, one of the most urgent needs of the hour is a thorough spring-cleaning of some vital terms. They have become so overlaid with the traditions of men that their original texture is forgotten and their meaning obscure. The term the Kingdom of God is one of them. It is used sometimes glibly and sometimes vaguely, with no attempt at definition. Everybody is supposed to know by instinct what it is and means. Yet few take the trouble to seek its meaning, and are not told by those whose duty it is to instruct. In the proposed basis of union of the Congregational, Methodist and Presbyterian Churches of South Africa, it is used vaguely with no attempt at definition. Many quote our Lord's words: "The Kingdom of God is within you" (*Luke* 17:21), and understand them to mean the kingdom is an inner, subjective experience without objective reality, that is, the kingdom is something in our own hearts. Long ago, the learned Dean Alford pointed out the impossibility of such a meaning. Our Lord was addressing the Pharisees, His bitter and constant enemies. If the Kingdom of God was in their hearts, why the long and calculated hostility to the King? [32] Later, our Lord said to them, "The Kingdom of God shall be taken from you, and given to a NATION bringing forth the fruits thereof" (*Matthew* 21:43). "And when the chief priests and Pharisees

---

[32]"The misunderstanding which rendered these words '*within you*,' meaning this in a spiritual sense, '*in your hearts*,' should have been prevented by reflecting that they are addressed to the Pharisees, in whose hearts it certainly *was* not." Dean Alford in *The Greek Testament With A Critically Revised Text: A Digest Of Various readings: Marginal References To Verbal And Idiomatic Usage: Prolegomena: And A Critical And Exegetical Commentary* Dean Henry Alford, DD. (Rivingtons, London, 1856)

N.B. In the Revised Version of the bible, the marginal rendering of the word is 'among'.

had heard his parables, they perceived that he spoke of them" (verse 45). How could a personal experience be taken away, and how could it be transferred to a nation? The word *nation* implies a constituted, organised authority for administration. Then again, it is frequently said the Church is the kingdom. There is no Scriptural authority for such a statement.

A kingdom implies a king to rule or reign, a body of subjects, and a constitution regulating the life and activities of the monarch and his people. While the kingdom is the Kingdom of God, the "Father judgeth no man but hath committed all judgement unto the Son" (*John* 5:22), Who at the end shall deliver up the kingdom to God, "that God may be all in all" (1 *Corinthians* 15:24-28). The constitution is that body of laws, statutes, judgements and ordinances given originally by God and ratified by our Lord Jesus Christ. As was pointed out in section 26, that constitution is concerned mainly with life on this material plane. The Kingdom is to be universal, ultimately, as we learn from *Daniel* 7:4, *Psalm* 72 and many other Scriptures, but its beginning is with a selected people. It should be noted that in speaking of the kingdom, our Lord invariably uses the present tense. He never says the Kingdom of God will be; it *is*, and it *is* like.... The kingdom was established on Sinai (*Exodus* 19), and is in existence still. It is not functioning as it should and will, for the kingdom suffereth violence, and the violent take it by force. "For the wicked doth compass about the righteous; therefore wrong judgement proceedeth" (*Habakkuk* 1:4). The Babylonian system has been imposed upon the world, but the day of reckoning is at hand. Jesus never taught us to pray for the creation of the Kingdom of God: He taught us to pray for its coming. Already it impinges upon this mundane world and is ready to burst through. Nevertheless, "Thus saith the Lord God; I will yet *for* this be enquired of by the house of Israel, to do it for them" (*Ezekiel* 36: 37).

Because we have lost the vision of the impending Messianic reign on earth we have floundered into the morass, and men have lost hope of righting the wrongs of life. "Where there is no vision the people perish" (*Proverbs* 29:18). The Church sings its great sigh in the words:

"Thy Kingdom come, O Lord,
Thy rule, O Christ, begin;
Break with Thine iron rod
The tyrannies of sin.
Where is Thy reign of peace
And purity and love?
When shall all hatred cease,
As in the realms above?"[33]

The above wistful questions will soon be answered. The weary, torn and bleeding world has not much longer to wait for the coming of the Kingdom. That the Kingdom of God relates to life on this material plane the Scriptures make clear. We have only to read such passages as *Isaiah* 65, *Amos* 9:14, *Matthew* 6:32 and *Revelation* 21. The listening ear can catch the rumbling, distant sounds of the approach of the King. "The Lord God shall give unto him the throne of his father David: and he shall reign over the house of Jacob for ever: and of his kingdom there shall be no end" (*Luke* 1:33).

The vision of the coming Kingdom must not be attenuated into a nebulous something unrelated to material needs; the Kingdom established by God at Sinai is to "come" as an ordered society on earth with Christ, the Anointed, as actual reigning Monarch. Then, and then only, shall we see God's will done on earth as it is done in heaven. The exultant shout of the heavenly host, like the shout of peers at the Queen's Coronation, will yet be heard: "The sovereignty of the world now belongs to our Lord and His Christ; and He

---

[33] Words by Frederick Hosmer, 1905

will be King until the ages of the ages" (*Revelation* 11:15, *Weymouth*).

30

WE BELIEVE IN THE PERSONAL RETURN OF OUR LORD AS KING, as well as in His return as "The Apostle and High Priest of our profession." The Bible abounds in references to the Messiah (to use the Hebrew form) and the Christ (to use the Greek form) and His Kingdom. Such passages as *Psalm* 72 and *Daniel* 7:9-28 are among those which immediately spring to mind. Nowhere is there any evidence that the kingdom expressed or implied in these and kindred passages means anything but what is usually connoted by the term. Such words as "The Lord God shall give unto him the throne of his father David" (*Luke* 1:32), rule out all ideas of a nebulous Utopia unrelated to the practical affairs of life. It is a Kingdom in which social, economic, political and religious activities play their part according to the Divine conception. We see only a travesty of these things now. When the King comes we shall see them lifted to that higher level which God intended and designed.

We need to think in terms of national life as well as in terms of individual life. We are in danger of losing the vision of the majesty of Christ, yet the Scriptures abound in figures of regal splendour. "When the Son of man shall come in his glory... then shall he sit on the throne of his glory; and before him shall be gathered all nations.... Then shall the King say unto them..." (*Matthew* 25:31-34). Here we see the King in state exercising that function of judgement which He declared the Father had committed unto Him (*John* 5:22). While we have come to associate this with the judgement of individuals, the address itself, as recorded in the passage above referred to, is clearly related to nations, whatever individual application it may have. There we see Christ seated on His throne, not as the Saviour of the individual soul, but as the King and Judge of "all nations." Moreover, the judgement is pronounced not on the ground of spiritual, or emotional, experience, but on the ground of concrete actions in relation to material needs. "I was an hungered, and ye gave me meat: I was thirsty, and ye gave me drink..." (*Matthew* 25:35). To this throne He "comes" as was pre-visioned in *Daniel* 7. It would be straining language beyond all legitimate use to say this implies anything but a personal coming. We cannot conceive of an influence occupying a throne and pronouncing judgement, however potent and widespread the influence may be.

31

WE BELIEVE IN THE PRE-MILLENNIAL COMING OF THE KING, that is, that the King will come before the Millennium begins. But for a tendency in some quarters to strain both the facts and the language beyond legitimate use and meaning, it would not be necessary to remark on the distinction between the pre-Millennial Coming and a post-Millennial return. [34] Yet there are sincere and earnest Christians who think His coming can be only after the Millennium. What is meant by the Millennium? Chambers' Etymological Dictionary defines it as "A thousand years: the thousand years during which, as some believe, Christ will personally reign on the earth." It might be contended that Christ could reign on the earth without being personally present, but the many Scriptures which state in unequivocal terms that He will personally come make such a contention unwarranted. The world needs Him to enforce His will. He is alive to-day, as the late Doctor Dale[35] came to realise on that memorable day in his study, and the earth is still His. All authority has been given unto Him, but the world treats Him as an absentee landlord and scoffs at His claims. Such parables as that of "A certain nobleman who went into a far country to receive for himself a kingdom and to return" (*Luke*

---

[34] "The majority both in number, and in learning and research, adopt the pre-millennial advent: following, as it seems to me, the plain and undeniable sense of the sacred text itself." Dean Alford op.cit *The Greek Testament, etc: Prolegomena*: viii, par. 11.
[35] Dr. R.W. Dale, Pastor of Carrs Lane Church, Birmingham (1854 – 1895)

19:12), make it abundantly clear that the King has not abdicated; He will require of His stewards an account of their stewardship. Their tenure of office is expressed in the words: "Occupy till I come." They have no inherent right to the positions they fill. It is delegated authority which they exercise and there is a prescribed time-limit beyond which they cannot wield that authority. When the King returns, the seals of office must be handed in. "When he was returned, having received the kingdom, then he commanded these servants to be called unto him... that he might know how much every man had gained by trading." Here again we see the King administrating justice, not the Saviour offering mercy and grace. "Those mine enemies which would not that I should reign over them, bring hither and slay *them* before me." Against that judgement there is no appeal. It is pronounced by One to Whom has been given all authority in heaven and on earth.

32

WE BELIEVE IN THE HISTORICIST SCHOOL OF INTERPRETATION. There are four main schools of Prophecy interpretation. These are:

(1) The Historicist school.
(2) The Preterist school.
(3) The Futurist school.
(4) The Spiritualising school.

As its name implies, the Spiritualising school seeks to spiritualise all prophecy by making it apply to spiritual life and experience solely or mainly. We may thank God for those who sought to keep the faith alive during dark periods by finding spiritual hope and comfort in the promises of God. It cannot be gainsaid that the faith of the Church has been maintained by so doing when outward circumstances darkened the vision of the Messianic reign. Nor should we freely condemn those who prefer to dwell on the non-material side of truth. It always seems to me a tragedy when children outgrow their idealistic picture of Santa Claus. But we know they do. The facts of life compel them to surrender their nursery ideas. We know that childhood must give place to maturity, and few would deny that maturity is better than immaturity in a world of stern reality; and the hard facts of life refuse to accommodate themselves to the fancy of Santa Claus. Equally so, there are prophecies which will not yield their secret to any spiritualising theory. It is difficult to spiritualise land, and a nation, and a throne, and much of prophecy is concerned with these.

THE HISTORICIST SCHOOL of interpretation is that to which the Church has persistently held despite the attacks that have been made upon it. This school of interpretation regards prophecy as history written in advance. It accepts prophecy as the divine fore- and forth-telling of the outworking of certain principles which govern life. He Who sees the end from the beginning had told us in advance what developments would and will take place. Many of the things foretold do not represent the wish, or will, of God. The effect must follow the cause, as night follows day, but to announce the certain effects of stated causes is not the same thing as wishing those effects to materialise. God knows that evil will run its course. He knows that good will and must ultimately triumph. He knows the conflict between the two and the turmoil that must result from the conflict. "The wages of sin is death" (*Romans* 6:23). "Sin, when it is finished, bringeth forth death" (*James* 1:15). But "I have no pleasure in the death of him that dieth, saith the Lord God" (*Ezekiel* 18:32). Here we have the outworking of a given principle foreseen and foretold, but the result is the opposite of what the Foreteller would wish. A skilful doctor can forecast the various stages in the development of disease right up to the crisis. Shall we deny to God the wisdom and foreknowledge we concede to men? Prophecy is the voice of Divine Love warning men of the evil consequences of wrong choices, of selfishness, and of sin, and entreating them to seek good and pursue it in the certainty that, despite all opposition, good will triumph in the end. As the white and the red corpuscles in the blood contend for the mastery, so good and evil will contend. But the end is certain, however long the conflict may last.

> "For right is right since God is God,
> And right the day must win;
> To doubt would be disloyalty,
> To falter would be sin."[36]

Therefore, we regard prophecy as the divine foreshadowing of what will take place. What takes place becomes history. The major part of what was foreshown has already passed into history. On these grounds we believe the Historical school of interpretation is the right one, and we accept it as such.

33

THE HISTORICIST SCHOOL SEES IN ROME THE FOURTH EMPIRE and the fourth beast of Daniel's prophecies.[37] Consciously or unconsciously, certain Roman writers appear to have felt the words of the Prophet applied to imperial Rome. In the third century, Porphyry saw in the advance of the Church a threat to the Empire. Believing that the Christians derived their confidence from the Bible, particularly from the writings of Daniel, he set himself the task of discrediting the Prophet by attempting to prove that Daniel wrote after, and not before, the events he depicted. Porphyry wrote fifteen books against Christianity, most of which have not come down to us, but the Faith he set out to crush was adopted officially by the Empire within a few years of his death. In the early years of the fifth century Augustine, Bishop of Hippo, one of the Fathers of the Church, wrote in his *City of God*, "Two cities have been formed from two loves: the earthly from love of self, even to

---

[36] *The Right Must Win* Frederick William Faber (1814 –1863)
[37] *Daniel* 7:7; also vv.19-25

contempt of God; the heavenly from love of God, even to contempt of self. The earthly city has its highest representative in heathen Babylon and Rome." On the ruins of imperial Rome rose Rome papal, and the Church, on the basis of the Historical school of interpretation, saw in the papacy "that horn that had eyes, and a mouth that spoke great things," of *Daniel* 7, which made war with the saints, and 'the whore' of *Revelation*. Then arose the PRETERIST SCHOOL, for reasons which soon become obvious. "This view is said to have been first promulgated in anything like completeness by the Jesuit Alcasar, in his *Vestigatio arcani sensus in Apocalypsi*, published in 1614."[38] Preterist means past[39], and the votaries of this school taught that most of the prophecies, especially those relating to the persecution of the saints, had been fulfilled in earlier times. This was calculated to turn the eyes of the Church from the papacy, and to cease to regard that system as the one from which persecution would arise. To-day, Preterism belongs to the lumber-room of discarded things. It is hardly ever heard of. It wilted and perished in the fierce light of fact.

But the resources of the Jesuits were not exhausted. The FUTURIST SCHOOL of interpretation arose. If we are to believe Dean Alford, this, too, was started by Jesuits. "The founder of this system in modern times (the Apostolic Fathers can hardly with fairness be cited for it, seeing that for them all was future) appears to have been the Jesuit Ribera, about AD 1580."[40] Supporters of this school transfer most of the *Book of Revelation* to the future. Many earnest Christians have adopted this theory apparently without due regard to its implications. The Futurist school requires a gap in Daniel's seventieth week. Hence arises "the gap theory," that is, after the cutting off of the Messiah in the midst of the seventieth week history stands in a state of suspended animation. The balance of the week is to find its fulfilment in the future when

---

[38] op.cit. *The Greek Testament, etc: Prolegomena*: viii, v, 3a

[39] from L. *praeteritus – praeter*, beyond, and *eo, itum*, to go. *Chambers Etymological Dictionary* (repr.1932.) Also, **preterite**, one expressing past action or state; past, bygone. *The Concise Oxford Dictionary* (repr.1949)

[40] op.cit. *The Greek Testament, etc: Prolegomena*: viii, v, 15.

the great things depicted in apocalyptic Scriptures will be fulfilled in a few brief years. British-Israelites see no justification for such a theory. The prophecies concerning the last two thousand years have been fulfilled. They are in strict accord with the prophecy given to St. John by Jesus Christ, as interpreted by the Historicist school. It confirms our faith that prophecy is history written in advance.

34

The previous pages have shown that British-Israelites base their faith and teaching entirely on the Bible, and they accept the Scriptures with unquestioning confidence and trust. They accept the historical Creeds of the Church without mental reservations. They would scorn to confess with their lips while in their hearts and minds denying the things they affirm to be true. They are reverently loyal to the fundamental doctrines of the Protestant Church, and desire to declare the whole counsel of God. They seek to live in love and charity with all who love our Lord Jesus Christ, and are ready to co-operate with all who strive to enthrone Him in the hearts of men and in the affairs of the nation and the world.

With so much in common with other organised bodies of believers two questions arise: What distinctive contribution to the life and thought of the Church has British-Israel teaching to offer? Is there any justification for a separate organisation?

In answering these questions it is necessary to state, first, what the British-Israel movement is not. It is not a sect, or denomination. It has no more wish to further rend the seamless robe of Christ than Wesley had, and only circumstances like those which drove his followers beyond the boundaries of the organised Church would impel its adherents to separate from existing Communions. Its aim is not to take people out of their churches; it would rather lead them back to the fold as vital and effective members of the Body of Christ.

The British-Israel movement has the aim of reinstating the Bible as the authoritative guide for the individual, the nation, and for the world. British-Israelites are a body of believers drawn from all Protestant churches, and some from the Roman Catholic Church, who feel the imperative need for the Church and the nation to listen to, to obey and do, whatever "Thus saith the Lord." The plaintive cry of God is pertinent to-day: "Thus saith the Lord, thy Redeemer, the Holy One of Israel; I am the Lord thy God which teacheth thee to profit, which leadeth thee by the way *that* thou shouldst go. O that thou hadst hearkened to my commandments! Then had thy peace been as a river and thy righteousness as the waves of the sea" (*Isaiah* 48:17-18). We have paid dearly for our failure to hearken. British-Israelites bear their testimony to the wisdom of listening to Him Who alone can teach to profit and lead in the right way. While the dogs of war are straining at the leash, God is offering the world the much desired peace, and we call on the world to hearken to those Commandments which will ensure the coveted end.

35

A distinctive note in the witness of the British-Israel teaching is its insistence on the duty of all who profess and call themselves Christians to accept the Bible as the inspired, authentic and authoritative Word of God written. We believe the Bible is a sufficient and authoritative guide on matters of faith and doctrine. We affirm that the Word of God is still the one sure lamp to the feet and light to the path for all who would walk in God's appointed ways, and that neither the individual nor the nation can escape from the maze of jumbled tracks until that Word is re-instated as the supreme guide in the individual and national life. We refuse to believe that the Bible is out of date, or superseded by "science falsely so called" (1 *Timothy* 6:20). We protest against "modernism" and (following the example of the late Professor Sayce[41] in regard to the 'critics') refuse to dignify it with a capital, on the ground that it saps the confidence of simple Christians in the Bible by placing the authority of scholarship above that of God's Word. We are fortified in this attitude by the knowledge that "modernism" is repeatedly compelled to surrender positions in which it thought it was safely entrenched. I mention a few instances only:

The spade is constantly bringing to light proof of Bible statements which "modernists" said were not true. Sir Charles Marston quotes *The New Commentary*, p. 194, as saying, in regard to the taking of Jericho, "The wall fell down flat is mere literary hyperbole intended to convey the completeness of the victory; and probably nobody would be more amazed than the actual writer to learn that his words were ever required as a point of faith to be understood literally. Had the walls collapsed entirely Rahab and her household could not have escaped."[42] But the excavations of Professor Garstang since 1930 show that the walls did fall flat. They are flat still.

The theory of the "modernists" that the Old Testament was a late production because, in earlier times, the people could not write, had to be given up when the Tel-el-Amarna tablets were unearthed. Further, excavations at Lachish in 1935 brought to light potsherds of Jeremiah's time inscribed with Hebrew writing in ink (cf. *Jeremiah* 36:18). There was found also a seal of Gedaliah, thus confirming the record in *Jeremiah* 40:7 that he was made governor. Both the potsherds and the seal I have seen and handled.

Owing to the discovery of *The New Babylonian Chronicle*,[43] the *Encyclopaedia Britannica* has had to correct itself. Bible Dictionaries, and even the British Museum, must do likewise in regard to the date of the fall of Nineveh. The history of the period was built up on the assumption that

---

[41] Rev. Prof. A.H. Sayce, DD. Fellow Of Queens College, Oxford, and Professor Of Assyriology (1845-1933)
[42] *The New Knowledge about the Old Testament*, Sir Charles Marston p.14.
[43] *New Babylonian Chronicle* translated by Mr. C. J. Gadd, M.A., Assistant in the Department of Egyptian and Assyrian Antiquities, British Museum, and is "Printed by order of the Trustees" of the museum.

Nineveh fell in 606 BC, and with its fall the Assyrian empire vanished. Both these "critical" facts prove to be fallacies. On that assumption, certain well-known Biblical events could not be fitted in, and, consequently, the Bible was judged to be wrong. The new discovery shows that Nineveh fell in 612 and not 606 BC, and the Biblical events now fall into place like the pieces of a jig-saw puzzle. The *New Babylonian Chronicle* has been translated by Mr. C. J. Gadd, M.A., Assistant in the Department of Egyptian and Assyrian Antiquities, British Museum, and is "Printed by order of the Trustees" of the Museum. Mr Gadd writes: "Everything which this Chronicle relates is entirely new... and the facts it states, even if not all the inferences it suggests, must be accepted without appeal, even though many of them are nothing less than revolutionary of opinions which have been most commonly held, and for which it seemed possible to quote very strong evidence" (p.3). Once again the inspired Word proves to be an impregnable rock against which the darts of the "critics" are powerless.

The disastrous effects of "modernistic" teaching are seen in the condition of the Church. The decline in ethical religion and the growth of sacerdotalism causes sorrow to lovers of the Church "which is His body." British-Israelites are among the chief mourners. They deplore the weakness of the Church and its inability to articulate the thoughts of God, in a time when moral and spiritual leadership is a clamant need. "By their fruits ye shall know them" is still the acid test, and by this test "modernism" stands condemned. In their opposition to "modernism," British-Israelites are not animated by personal feeling, but are moved by a deep concern for the welfare of the Church of God. For that reason they feel it is incumbent upon them to bear witness "to the word of his grace which is able to build you up" (*Acts* 20:32), and protest against the word of "modernism" which is so disastrously pulling down.

British-Israelites have implicit confidence in God's ability and willingness to fulfil literally all His gracious promises, and to honour all His commitments. Remembering that God said Israel should never "cease from being a nation before me for ever" (*Jeremiah* 31:36), they believe Israel as a nation, not as a Church, must be in existence still, for "God never goes back on his gifts and call." If it is in existence we should be able to find it, and to recognise it. It should be all the easier to do that since it was to be a great nation with a multitude of people. The section under Ephraim was to be "a multitude of nations" (*Genesis* 48:19), and the descendants of Jacob "a nation and a company of nations" (*Genesis* 35:11). "In the last days" the branches of Joseph were to "run over the wall," or to extend like a vigorous vine. It is impossible to conceal such a racial entity in such a world as ours. It can be identified by the divinely-appointed racial and functional marks, and those marks are borne by the British (Covenant) and allied peoples of today. We affirm that the manifold expressions in *The Book of Common Prayer* which connect the British people with "our forefather Abraham" are not accidental, nor chosen for mere euphony. They express a race consciousness embedded in the hearts of the people.

Remembering that God said the throne of David should be established for ever, that it should always be occupied by a descendant of David, and that ultimately our Lord should sit on that throne and reign over the house of Jacob for ever, British-Israelites believe that that throne is in existence still, and that its occupant must be a literal descendant of David; for "The Lord hath sworn *in* truth unto David: he will not turn from it; of the fruit of thy body will I set upon thy throne" (*Psalm* 132:11) . The British throne, and its monarch, meets the requirements of the case as shown in sections 13-15 above. With that conviction, British-Israelites call upon the monarch and the people to acknowledge their identity, and discharge their obligations of service to the world, that by so doing they may bring to fruition God's purpose in selecting and training the race to be a blessing to all nations, and to establish the earth (*Isaiah* 49:8).

37

THE KINGDOM MESSAGE occupies a prominent place in British-Israel teaching on the ground that it was so prominent in the teaching of our Lord. British-Israelites find that the bulk of his teaching centred on the Kingdom. The word *Kingdom* occurs 117 times in the four Gospels: Matthew uses it fifty times, Mark nineteen, Luke forty-four, and John four. Most of the parables have the Kingdom as their theme. On the other hand, the Church, *per se*, occupies an almost negligible place in His teaching as recorded in the Gospels. As the late Professor Hort pointed out, our Lord, according to the records, used the word *ecclesia* (Church) on only two occasions. The word *Church* occurs but three times in the Gospels, and Matthew is the only one to use it. Further, in the only prayer enjoined upon His followers by our Lord, the word *Church* does not occur, but the Kingdom is mentioned twice. In the presence of such a body of evidence there is no choice but to conclude that the *Kingdom* was the dominant thought in the mind of Jesus. The spread of sacerdotalism has confused the issue and we are frequently told by ecclesiastical leaders that the Church is the Kingdom. If the Church is the kingdom, why continue to pray for its coming? That the Church is here nobody will deny.

British-Israelites are far from belittling the Church and still farther from regarding it as a negligible institution. They believe the Church has a most honoured and honourable function to fill in the divine scheme of things, but to regard the Church and the kingdom as synonymous is to ignore the plain teaching of the Gospels, and to overlook the practical implications of the word *Kingdom.* This is not the place to discuss at length what the Church is and should be. I am simply stating the distinctive something in British-Israel teaching and, as mentioned above, that distinctive something is the Kingdom message.

A kingdom implies a king to rule or reign, a body of people to be governed, and a code of laws regulating the activities of the citizens and defining the mutual relations of the ruler and the ruled. An organised kingdom embraces all forms of corporate activity: social, economic, political (in the strict sense of the Greek word *politikos*, i.e. that which pertains to the policy to be followed in the interests of the citizen, *polites*), and religious. It is obvious that the church has no control over, and very little voice in regard to, the first three branches of corporate activity, and therefore can influence only a fraction of the life of the citizen. But God's "Kingdom ruleth over all" (*Psalm* 103:19).

Jesus never spoke of the coming or the establishment, of *a* kingdom. He used the definite article and spoke of *the* Kingdom, which implies something already in existence. To understand in detail His teaching about the kingdom would require a careful study of the Old Testament, and that lies outside the scope of this simple treatise. Brief reference to it has been made in sections 26-29. Jesus declared: "This gospel of the kingdom shall be preached in all the world for a witness to all nations; and then shall the end come" (*Matthew* 24:14). British-Israelites find in that pronouncement their charter for declaring the Kingdom message, and their justification for stressing the national side of that message.

38

Is there any need for a separate organisation to proclaim the foregoing Scriptural message? Unfortunately, the answer must be yes, qualified by the remark that there ought not to be. For some reason best known to themselves, for, as far as I am aware, it has never been made public, many ministers if the Churches condemn (surely in ignorance) the British-Israel message, despite its undiluted Scriptural content. At the same time, they tolerate, and sometimes seem to encourage, teaching that is un-scriptural and often subversive of the faith and doctrine of the Protestant Church. Intolerance, against which most of the existing denominations fought their way to freedom, has gripped the very bodies which formerly condemned it, and suffered under it.

39

In their desire to retain the faith once for all delivered to the saints, earnest souls sometimes ask: "How is it the Churches do not preach the British-Israel message?" My answer is: "If the Churches approved of any new movement of the Spirit of God in its initial stages there would be reason to question its truth. Speaking as a minister of, and lover of, the Church, I know it has been the unhappy fate of official religion to oppose any new spiritual movement at its beginning and, subsequently, has had to endorse and accept it. It would be unjust to my readers to make such a sweeping statement without supporting evidence. The informed reader will require nothing more than the following reminders:

In the days of His flesh, the question was asked concerning our Lord, "Have any of the rulers or of the Pharisees believed on Him?" (*John* 7:48). That, of course, was intended to be a crushing reproof to the foolish people who believed. But "the common people heard him gladly" (*Mark* 12:37). As to which were right, the rulers or the common people, history leaves no room for doubt;

In the fourteenth century, Wycliffe was ostracised, and compelled to resort to his 'poor preachers' to spread his message. Today he is honoured as 'The morning star of the Reformation';

In the sixteenth century, because he gave the people the Bible in their mother tongue, Tyndale was persecuted, hounded out of England, caught at Brussels and murdered. Today - what?

In the seventeenth century, Bunyan was imprisoned for many years for preaching the Word of God. Today, all the world reads his books, the Churches sing his hymns, and the Church which persecuted him has erected a magnificent stained-glass window to show how much he is honoured and loved;

In the eighteenth century, John Wesley vitalised England by his message, but was driven out of the Church which he loved. Is it necessary to say what the judgement of today is?

In the same century, Robert Raikes started the Sunday School Movement, against which the Assembly of the Church of Scotland warned its congregations;

In the nineteenth century, William Booth started the Salvation Army. He was greeted with rotten eggs. But the Church of England copied his example and started the Church Army;

In 1874 arose the Keswick Movement, of which the Revd. Prebendary Webb-Peplow writes as follows: "He was asked to meet a number of Evangelical clergymen to explain what it was all about. He told them that it was a movement for the deepening of spiritual life, and for teaching that God's grace is sufficient to enable us to overcome all sin. Whereon the chairman, a prominent Evangelical, exclaimed, 'Heresy, blasphemous heresy.' Today it is an honour to be on the Keswick platform."

In the light of the above, need we be surprised that British-Israelites find themselves cold-shouldered, and their faith condemned? They comfort themselves with the reflection that by standing among the officially condemned they are in a noble succession whose failures have proved most brilliant successes.

While recognising that the Church must be cautious, and perhaps conservative, I must remind its leaders of their duty to examine before pronouncing judgement. The wise words of Gamaliel apply to today: "...take heed to yourselves what ye intend to do as touching these men. For...if this counsel or this work be of men, it will come to nought: But if it be of God, ye cannot overthrow it; lest haply ye be found even to fight against God" (*Acts* 5:35 and 38-39).

*   *   *   *

"Now unto the King eternal, immortal, invisible, the only wise God, be honour and glory for ever and ever." (1 *Timothy* 1:17.)

End Notes:

The Balfour Declaration.

Foreign Office
November 2nd, 1917

Dear Lord Rothschild,

I have much pleasure in conveying to you. on behalf of His Majesty's Government, the following declaration of sympathy with Jewish Zionist aspirations which has been submitted to, and approved by, the Cabinet: His Majesty's Government view with favour the establishment in Palestine of a national home for the Jewish people, and will use their best endeavours to facilitate the achievement of this object, it being clearly understood that nothing shall be done which may prejudice the civil and religious rights of existing non-Jewish communities in Palestine, or the rights and political status enjoyed by Jews in any other country. I should be grateful if you would bring this declaration to the knowledge of the Zionist Federation.

Yours,
Arthur James Balfour

Index